Leaving Christianity to Follow Jesus

Aware Publishing
Fallbrook, CA 92028

First Aware Publishing softcover edition June 2016

ISBN: 978-0-9976411-0-3
E-Book ISBN: 978-0-9976411-1-0

To my daughter Kayla, whom I have not seen in many years. I miss you and hope this book reveals a little bit about who your dad is.

ACKNOWLEDGMENTS

My first readers, Lisa Thomas, Adam Green, Linda Kennedy, Donnie Hyde, Melissa Russler, and Astra Kelly.

Adam Green for being involved in the initial edits and forcing me to be a better writer.

Emily Sperling for editing the book and helping me to make it into something I am very proud of.

My family at Community of Faith Church that has shaped so much of what I know about following Jesus.

My wife Michelle and children Sophia and Roman for their encouragement and patience with me during the pursuit of my vocation, even when it was not easy for us.

A letter to my son Roman,

You are only nine years old as I write this, but I imagine you won't be reading it until you are an adult. I pray that as you grow older you will come to appreciate what I am sharing with you today.

I am writing in part to explain why your childhood is different from what the "other kids" have, as you and your sister so fondly remind your mother and me. Parenting comes with difficult decisions about how to raise children, especially when parents choose to go against what is mainstream. We have to make choices based on how we think the future will unfold, hoping these decisions lead to what is best for our children-- what is best for you. If the future we foresee does not come to pass, we are faced with all sorts of criticism. So do we parents risk doing what we believe to be right, or do we settle for what "everyone else" is doing? That way, at least, we will have failed side-by-side with the majority.

This letter and the following book is to explain that I have chosen the riskier path of doing what I believe to be right. One day, when you are grown and have learned more of life, I hope to hear what you think of the choices I am making today. At the very least, I hope that my example to stay true to what I believe will empower you to make your own decisions--ones where you do not blindly follow the way of the crowd.

Within our family, I am given the task of living out the disciple's walk before you. There is no pretending at home. You get to see me when I am strong and when I am weak. There will be no fooling you. I wonder how you will evaluate my witness when you look back on it from adulthood. Will my witness be a help or a hindrance to you? I hope to teach you what mercy looks like because I will surely need it. Being a follower of Jesus is not about being perfect; I will make mistakes, and I will sin. What being a follower of Jesus does mean is that we have a way to name sin, a way to confess it, and a way to both offer and receive forgiveness. We should always be maturing in our faith and working to develop godly character that directs us away from sin—but no matter how far we come, we will never grow out of our need for forgiveness.

I love you son,
              Dad

CONTENTS

Part One

Eyes to See

"By this everyone will know that you are my disciples, if you have love for one another."

- Jesus

INVITATON

It is odd what can capture one's attention in a moment of emotional turmoil. For me, it is the feel and sound of the graveled path crunching beneath my shoes, and the odd combination of pine and palm trees on either side of me. The air smells like Summer. The path opens into a clearing that is enclosed by a wall of tropical vegetation, purple and red flowers spotting the dense foliage. It feels completely isolated from the rest of the world. I make my way through the clearing and past the gathering crowd, taking my place behind the podium. The gentle splashing of the ornamental waterfall behind me is barely audible over the low hum of the patient crowd before me.

Even with the heat, the people have gathered. The organizers had set up seats for two hundred and fifty guests, but there have to be over three hundred people in attendance. I will never forget this day.

The whole situation seems surreal. I have to concentrate on my breathing as I feel anger grip me, creating a different kind of heat inside. Now is not the time for that. Now is the time for compassion. I am about to offer a prayer on behalf of a dear friend and pastor, Brad. He was only fifty-seven. It has been over six weeks since his death and we still do not know the cause of it. His widow is convinced he died of a broken heart. No matter the cause, the events that have led up to this moment should never have happened. Disagreements in church are not supposed to end with someone's death.

I had met Brad three years earlier while introducing myself to other pastors in town. I was impressed that Brad didn't view Christianity as a competition between churches, as I had seen all too often. Despite our differences in theology, he was comfortable working with me. He served a church where the previous pastor retired after a fifteen-year ministry. When a church has had a pastor for so long, the congregation becomes used to the way things have "always" been. That sort of situation is hard for a pastor to walk into. I was not privy to the initial issues between Brad and some members of his congregation, but there were some serious missteps that took place on both sides. When it was evident that the situation was escalating, it became time for the denominational leaders to step in and moderate the disagreements; but they did not come, which allowed the situation to fester for years. A group formed to drive Brad out of office. It was only after Brad had died that any resources or personnel came from the denomination to teach the church how to process disagreements and conflict.

As much as I love Brad, I believe there were real issues and a sense of injustice for those who had a problem with him. The disgruntled parties had no good way to address their concerns except through Brad. What was lacking through this ordeal was a desire for reconciliation and a goal to work for peace. That desire may have been there in the beginning, but burned out as the situation progressed. Still, the denomination officials focused more on causing as little damage to the church rather than reconciliation or holding the members involved accountable for their actions in light of their Christian vows.

Brad had told me that he was going to ask to be reassigned to a different church because the situation was so draining. I counseled him to look at things differently. I told him that it was clear that there was real pain, suffering, and anger on both sides of the situation. It would be easy to walk away, but the problem would still remain. Jesus said that his followers would be known for their love of one another. The ability for Jesus' followers to resolve problems by the practice of confession, forgiveness, and reconciliation will ultimately enable the world to recognize that Jesus was sent from God. If a church cannot resolve its issues, what business does it have inviting anyone to join its fellowship? Reconciliation is what being a Christian is about. Learning how to love one another even when we step on each other's toes. This is how disciples are formed: by doing the hard work of the Gospel.

Following this advice requires a system that holds believers accountable to their convictions—not by legalistic control, but by serving as a reminder of whom we have committed ourselves to be, especially in the midst of pain. People need help to stay committed to their convictions and make right decisions. But this system did not exist in Brad's church.

There was no reconciliation. There was no accountability to Christian vows. There was no commitment to practice confession and forgiveness. The offended parties were not successfully brought together to work through their grievances. Consequently, a small group from the denomination met behind closed doors and made decisions for the whole community—decisions that the denominational group did not have to answer for. Rather than choosing to resolve the issues, they chose to remove Brad, believing that to be the best option for the church. The end result was that Brad would not be returning to his church, nor any church within that denomination.

No one at the local church was given a clear answer as to why Brad was ousted, not even his wife. The group stated that to protect Brad's privacy they could not discuss the matter. Brad was just as confused and hurt as the rest of us. Some members of the church were happy with the decision, while others left the denomination over how the situation was handled. Apparently the church was supposed to heal without reconciliation between parties.

In the end, the local church continued with nothing resolved. People just moved on. No confession. No forgiveness. No reconciliation. No witnesses to the world that there is good news for those in pain and suffering.

As for Brad, in light of needing to begin a new career and being an avid scuba diver, he decided to get his diving instructor's certification. It was this new pursuit that brought about the circumstances of Brad's death. He hoped to start a dive club and leave the pain of the church behind. Brad died fewer than two weeks later while qualifying for his certification. Many assumed it was an aneurism or heart attack at the time; however, it was due to an obscure heart issue that took months after his death for the doctors to discover.

It is events such as what happened between Brad and his congregation that have left Christians doubting the claims of their faith. After seeing what was done to Brad, many of us were completely disillusioned with the workings of organized religion and the failure to address the real needs of the church. Aren't we, as Christians, supposed to be different from the corporate, bureaucratic, and demeaning behavior we find all around us? Many non-Christians see this kind of treatment between followers and are grateful not to have anything to do with Christianity. The core of the problem surrounding the events of Brad's death is linked to differing ideas of what Christianity is, and how to live as a Christian.

What is Christianity?

How would you define the word "Christian"? How would you summarize what Christians believe? You likely have at least a partial answer to these questions—and that is a problem. I cannot use the word "Christian" without bringing to mind everything you already know about Christianity, and what the word means to you is likely not the same as it is for the next ten people I ask. Take a moment to think about all the different examples of Christians in the media. Is being a Christian defined by the hateful rants and ravings of the Westboro Baptist Church, or the old world tranquility of the Amish? Conservative evangelicals who support the military, or movements promoting nonviolent love of enemies like The Simple Way? Mega churches promising prosperity, or monks living without private ownership of anything? Each of these groups claim to be Christian, but how are these even the same religion? With contrasting and often conflicting claims, is it surprising that a common word used to describe Christians is "hypocrite"? Many find Christians to be judgmental, divisive, and ignorant.

I am a follower of Jesus, but why would I want to call myself a Christian? Why would I want to be associated with a group where many are perceived to be practicing hate, greed, and violence in the name of Christ? The Jesus I know does not fit into popular understandings of Christianity. I know many who have rejected the faith due to the horrible example set by some claiming to represent Jesus. In this book I want to re-present the religion of Jesus free from the baggage of Christianity.

I am leaving Christianity to follow Jesus.

I am not saying there are no true followers of Jesus within Christianity; there are many. Nor am I rejecting everything Christians believe. What I am saying is that nothing commonly believed in Christianity is beyond question simply because it has traditional or historic use in the church. The distortions of the faith and the unnecessary complexity of Christian doctrine are leading to the collapse of Christianity. We need to clear the slate and start fresh. To get back to the roots and allow the original Jesus to confront us again with his call to radical faithfulness. I refer to the radical way of Jesus as the Sacred Revolution.

Call to Revolution

We have been lulled to sleep. It is time to wake up. The way of Jesus goes beyond a personal, private relationship with God. It is a call for change, for us to look at the way the world is currently ordered. Those who rule by oppression and brutality are pretenders and we are called to deny their authority and demands for allegiance. All people are created in the image of God and any system that rules as a hierarchy, in which some benefit at the expense of the many, is false and opposes God. It is time to take action.

There is a Sacred Revolution happening. We are rejecting the accepted principles and challenging the given ideologies of how our world and our religion is structured. We believe that there is a Creator who has not abandoned creation, and we are choosing to live by the principles of Jesus. We believe that Jesus' actions and teachings are the clearest expression of what God is actually like, and we are summoned to his way of life as disciples. The way of Jesus is a revolution on a personal, cultural, and political level. Ours is a sacred revolution, conducted with love for the sake of peace using nonviolent confrontation.

Following Jesus comes with great risk. Are you ready to be fearless in uncovering the falsehoods of the current social order? Are you ready to break away from the consumerist lifestyle and adopt a new way of life consistent with God's vision for the world? Everything a revolutionary does needs to be in service to God's vision and in solidarity with our sisters and brothers. Our actions are no longer our own. Everything we do will be seen as representing God to the world.

We renounce violence, choosing only nonviolent action. This is a great threat to systems of domination. Those in positions of authority gain their ultimate power from people who are willing to kill, maim, and imprison in the name of that authority. If there is a sudden outbreak of people refusing to kill, then those in authority lose their power. Power is never relinquished easily. As nonviolent revolutionaries, we can expect consequences from those who are challenged by our commitment to preserving life.

The Sacred Revolution is voluntary and needs people who are fully committed to God's vision for the world. What follows is your guide for joining the Sacred Revolution.

VISION AND MISSION

In the Sacred Revolution, everyone is on the front line. We each need to know our role and what is expected of us or else we will be working against the revolution. It is natural to desire clear, step-by-step instructions in order to feel confident in our actions. We all know what happens to the best laid plans—according to the poem by Robert Burns, they often go awry. Hence the military saying, "no plan survives contact with the enemy."

I am providing you with a clear vision of our goal and the revolution's top three priorities. The vision and priorities are rules and parameters that guide our thinking and actions. Armed with this knowledge, we can improvise appropriately in any given situation, becoming far more flexible and effective than if we had tried to memorize a list of dos and don'ts.

You have probably listened to music or seen sheet music at some point in your life. Perhaps you have even performed. In music there are rules to learn, such as where each note can be found on an instrument, and how each note works with the timing of the musical composition. While these rules may initially seem limiting or controlling, they liberate the performer and allow them to create incredible beauty. When more than one person is playing, then the rules allow the two to work in harmony, free and yet bound by similar understandings. The possibilities are endless.

Mastery of musical rules and the ability to work with fellow performers allows musicians to improvise. Their playing appears to be random but is evidence that they have internalized the rules and no longer need to use the same kind of concentration they once did. Musicians can move us to experience extreme emotion and personal transcendence. This is the same kind of internalized mastery and understanding we utilize when it comes to the rules of the

Sacred Revolution. Once these rules are part of who we are and how we think, we are able to create great beauty with our lives, transforming the world, and bringing others to an experience of wholeness and interconnectedness.

By focusing on learning the vision and the top three priorities, Sacred Revolutionaries and their Sacred Communities can exist anywhere, working for the common good even when we cannot be physically connected. A distributed network of Sacred Communities is harder to stop by those who would wish us harm. The importance of the vision and priorities of the revolution cannot be overstated.

As I share God's vision for humanity with you, keep in mind that I cannot explain everything at once. I need to start with a basic idea so you can wrap your head around the whole concept. I will fill out the details of the vision as I go through the rest of this book. For now, here is the basic idea:

Life is the most amazing gift you will ever receive. Many, however, would not describe their lives as a gift. People whose lives consist of endless hunger or random acts of violence; lives with no security, where death is more real than happiness; for them, they may rightfully ask, "Why? Why was I created? How is this life a gift?"

God is relentlessly concerned with life—life set free from those who oppress and brutalize. Life set free from isolation and shame. Life set free from disease and sorrow. Life experienced in abundance and joy, beauty and peace: wholeness on a universal scale.

The biblical word for this universal wholeness is shalom. Often shalom is translated as "peace," but it means so much more than that. Our world thinks of peace as an end to fighting, but believes that to gain peace one must use violence to destroy or overwhelm the enemy. Peace as it relates to shalom is achieved through justice and reconciliation. The fighting stops because each side no longer desires to battle. Our world's version of peace leaves enemies in its wake who rise up over and over again with the desire to rekindle ancient grievances. Shalom seeks for everyone to be reconciled with each other, leaving only friends.

In addition to peace, shalom refers to abundance. Shalom exists when God's desire that "there should be no one in need among you" is fulfilled. There is abundance for all because people have finally learned to share. Creation and life are respected as there is a return to true humanity. Shalom is a one-word summary of God's vision for all of creation. This one word brings to mind the vision of a world brought to its intended harmony and beauty.

Shalom is the vision of the revolution and it is hard to contain. How do we work with something so all-encompassing? Begin by imagining our world shaped by shalom. There is little to draw from in our everyday experience. Imagine instead something you know, like the town or city you live in with all its good and bad. Now change what you see by imagining what the people would be like if their lives and our world was shaped by shalom:

Imagine the absence of a police force or jail system—they are unnecessary. You see a people willing to take the time to untangle misunderstandings rather than jump to conclusions and judgments. A people filled with concern for one another to the extent that they ensure no one goes without basic needs like food, a safe warm place to stay, friendship, and a meaningful vocation.

It sounds unbelievable. For anything that is ruining this image for you, ask yourself if those problems would be solved if everyone had their personal needs met and honestly desired to work out misunderstandings. What if everyone had a greater sense of connectedness?

Imagine the air and water clean, with human industry working in cooperation with nature. Cities are beautiful places that lack ghettos or projects of any kind. The challenges facing people are no longer crime, racism, or violence. Instead, people are challenged to perfect their art and music and focus on exploration and education. Immerse your mind in this world shaped by shalom and focus on it until its reality can be seen—no matter how unbelievable it may sound right now.

Once you can see this vision, think about its key attributes.

- Shalom involves our world rather than forming an artificial escape to somewhere else, like heaven.
- Shalom teaches reconciliation over retribution.
- Shalom is about caring for those most in need.

With these three attributes in mind, we can start evaluating how our actions relate to them. How do our daily activities impact the ecology of our world? Are we learning how to practice reconciliation in the conflicts of our lives? Do we have a concern for those in need and do we take action to resolve those concerns? By asking questions like these, it shows how a vision of the goal is more helpful than a list of dos and don'ts. It is much more adaptable to different situations you may find yourself in.

Let me insert a word of caution here: this vision of shalom is of the ideal state which is nearly impossible to obtain with the way we live today. For example, almost every activity we partake in has an adverse impact on the environment, from driving a car to church to using a tablet to write a book. Do not let these thoughts paralyze you. We have to start somewhere. The point is to be aware of what is wrong and what we can do to move in the right direction. We need to first accept that we live in a gray zone rather than a clearly defined black and white world. In many respects, we are going to be in an ongoing state of reforming from our own hypocrisy. Give up the guilt of not being perfect. The Sacred Revolution is a process of becoming.

To utilize the vision, begin to internalize a clear image of shalom in your mind, just as a musician would internalize a song in order to perform it. After this we will build on that vision by learning how to implement the top three priorities of the revolution. These priorities are how an individual's desires are transformed in order to bring about shalom. God cannot bring about shalom alone, as it requires cooperation from us and a willingness and desire to live God's vision. Without this cooperation, God would be just another tyrant enforcing an all-powerful will upon unwilling subjects. To try and enforce shalom on anyone would immediately destroy the intention of God's vision.

The Sacred Revolution's Top Three Priorities

Gratitude
A proper sense of gratitude is the source of our motivation for everything we do in the revolution. As it is the most important priority, a whole section of this book is dedicated solely to the understanding of gratitude and how to develop it in one's life.

Covenantal Faithfulness
A covenant is an agreement in which different parties bind themselves to each other. The most familiar example of a covenant today is marriage. In a typical marriage, two parties agree to bind themselves to one another with certain obligations and expectations and their agreement is witnessed before God. The idea of covenantal faithfulness is the act of keeping those obligations and expectations. Our covenant with God covers our relationship with God, each other, and all of creation.

The Latin word for covenant is "testament," which is how we refer to the whole of scripture: The Old and New Testaments. This demonstrates how significant covenant is to the entire Bible. The reason covenant is so significant is because it defines what the transformation needs to look like in people's lives in order to bring about shalom. Covenant defines right relationships between God, each other, and creation. Our learning and keeping of the covenant is a top priority in working towards God's vision of shalom. We will explore this topic more generally in part two of this book.

Community

Learning how to live in community is a demonstration of what the Sacred Revolution is meant to look like. It is one thing for you, as an individual, to experience gratitude and focus on your part of the covenant, but if that does not translate into deeper connections and interdependence with other Revolutionaries, then we have failed to bring about tangible transformation—a demonstration that another way of life is possible.

What the world needs, and what the vision of shalom is all about, are new ways for people to live together in life-affirming ways. We need examples of communities that can handle hurting each other's feelings and having meaningful disagreements. If we proclaim peace through reconciliation and restoration then we need to be able to implement that within our communities. We need to know how to share, be more interdependent, and provide for those in need within our faith community. In short, we need to model a little taste of shalom in the present. This is our most powerful witness to the world. Whatever we try to tell the world will fall on deaf ears unless they can see it genuinely lived out. We will explore several ways we can work on this throughout this book.

Summary of the Vision and Mission

God's vision for creation, and the goal of the Sacred Revolution, is shalom: a world brought to its intended state of beauty, abundance, and reconciled relationships. Our top priorities are to practice gratitude, grow in covenantal faithfulness, and be examples of the shalom way of life through living communities.

DOMINATION SYSTEM

The Sacred Revolution concerns the social, political, and economic arrangements of society, as well as personal transformation and healing. However, we have a tendency to think of religion as primarily a private and personal matter. We want to compartmentalize the spiritual so that it is not soiled by the dirtiness of politics. In reality, there is no division between religion and any other aspects of life such as the social, political, and economic.

Religion
Religion at its core is a collection of stories that explain what life is all about, how life should be lived, what is right and wrong, and why things are the way they are. These explanations of how to live life are not always called religion—they may be called an economic theory or a political philosophy. No matter what they are called, these stories paint a picture of the world that explains why a people follow a certain social structure. The Sacred Revolution requires a deeper look into societal norms. It is a call to resist brutality, protect life, celebrate beauty, and experience true community. It creates a link between the social, political, and economic realities of life, as it brings into question the existing social order and the religion that supports it.

Social Order
Social order, or social arrangements, come with a cost that individuals must pay. For example, if people are going to drive cars we need laws. Traffic laws are a type of social arrangement that determines behavior on the road, from which side of the street to drive on to what traffic lights mean. As is the case with traffic laws, it is clear why certain social arrangements are in place, but not so for others. Why do some people have more money than they could ever use

without having to work, while others who work hard do not have enough money for food and health care? How a culture explains and justifies these social arrangements is the role of religion.

Understanding the Religion of the United States

Domination System
Along your journey in the Sacred Revolution is a term you will need to understand: Domination System. These two words are used to describe cultures arranged in a hierarchical fashion in which the few benefit at the expense of the many. Walter Wink, a theologian and scholar who has written extensively on the study of nonviolence, defined the Domination System as:

> A world-encompassing system characterized by unjust economic relations, oppressive political relations, patriarchal gender relations, prejudiced racial or ethnic relations, hierarchical power relations, and the use of violence to maintain them; in short, "civilization."

Should the United States be considered a domination system? At first glance, it may seem the principles the United States is founded on are in complete opposition to domination. We celebrate the freedom of the individual, protect the rights of minorities, and provide opportunity to those who work hard and play by the rules. We call ourselves a democracy because we believe everyone should have a voice in how things are run. We believe inequalities between individuals should be based on merit. If someone has more of something, it should be because they have worked harder. Merit means what someone has is a result of having earned it. Based on these principles, the United States is anything but a domination system.

We need only look at our past to prove that our country's structure is built not on a foundation of principles, but of its actions. Until recently, it was only the white-male landowner's rights and opportunities that the United States protected. For most of American history, women and children were viewed as property. The United States was the cause of twenty million Native Americans losing their lives during the genocidal conquest of North America (Pinker, 2011:195), and the inhuman conditions that the Africans, Chinese, and Irish suffered from slavery and racism. Eighteen million Africans died in the slave trade (Pinker, 2011:195). White male landowners had no cause to see the United States as a Domination System, but their view would differ greatly from that of women, African slaves, and Native Americans.

The United States has taken important steps in the right direction to address the atrocities of the past. Slavery has been abolished. Rights have been granted to minorities, women, and children. But there is a long road ahead of us— while we have worked on resolving and healing our past, a new and potentially greater threat still exists. It arose in the 70s and continues to grow today: wealth inequality. Wealth enables freedom and opportunity in our capitalistic culture. However, when wealth inequality becomes too great, freedom and opportunity for all is threatened.

In this chapter, I will discuss economic structures and statistics. You can learn more about what I discuss from *Social Problems and the Quality of Life*, Thirteenth Edition by Robert H. Lauer and Jeanette C. Lauer. Information that does not come from *Social Problems and the Quality of Life* will be cited at the end of this section.

Economics
If people were fully informed about how our economic system works and how it contains inherent injustice, they would never stand for it. Those who control the wealth

intentionally conceal the way things work and perpetuate the confusion around economics to maintain this ignorance of the system. If someone feels it is beyond their ability to understand how economics works, then they will not bother to ask questions. We need to understand how the system works if we are to have any ability to ask critical questions or propose change; otherwise we will continue to be kept in the dark, controlled by our ignorance. The life our children inherit depends on our willingness to stretch ourselves to become informed.

Simply asking the questions is it working or is there growth is not sufficient when it comes to making economic policy. Cancer grows but it is not life supporting. The body does not recognize it as a deformity of life. The cancer grows but is self-serving and ultimately unsustainable, causing the death of the body. A society is a social body. As a body we have to be able to discern the difference between life-affirming growth and the deformities that will destroy us. It is not enough for someone to demonstrate that a policy or system works. We need to know that it supports what we need for life and health. If the growth comes at the expense of the necessities of life (such as water, air, food, or safety), then it will kill us in the end. How should we evaluate the growth our culture is currently experiencing? To do that we need to clear away some of the mystery of capitalism and class structure in the United States.

Class and Capital in the United States

Our society is structured as a hierarchy divided by class. Classes are ways to rank where people fall according to their levels of income. Here is a way of defining who falls into which class:

> Lower Class: The bottom 50% of the population are the lower or working class. The median family income for

the United States is fifty thousand dollars per year. Half of the United States' families falls below this level.

Middle Class: This comprises the next 40% of the population. These families do better than the majority but have yet to make it into the upper class.

Upper Class: The next 9% of the population defines the Upper Class. These families define our culture's definition of wealthy, bringing home approximately three hundred eighty thousand dollars or more per year.

Elite Class: At the very top is the remaining 1%. These individuals or families make over one million dollars per year.

Defining Earned and Unearned Income
There are two main types of income: earned income as the result of labor, and unearned income as the result of owning capital (assets) and renting it out. Capital can be land, buildings, or money, where rent on money is called interest. It is important to understand the distinction between earned and unearned income because of their differences.

Earned income increases as a result of the growth of the economy. There are several tactics to increase income, such as advancing in job position (often requiring additional education), or by working harder, longer, or receiving a raise. These tactics take time and are dependent on how well the economy is doing. If the economy is down, raises are often postponed. Studies show that the economy grows approximately 2% to 3% per year.

Unearned income increases with the returns gained from owning capital. This is a collection of all income from all owned capital, such as rents, dividends, and profits. The money from rents are based on rates of return that are typically 5% which is greater than the growth of the economy at 2% to 3%. This means that people in possession of capital are in a position to grow their income faster than those earning income from labor. If this is allowed to continue, the percentage of capital will be consolidated by an increasingly smaller portion of the population.

Learning Capitalism from Monopoly®

The game Monopoly® teaches children the difference between earned and unearned income. By passing "GO" you receive a paycheck of two hundred dollars—your set salary. This is earned income from labor. If you choose to acquire properties or utilities to collect capital, you now have another source of income—rent. This is unearned income. As other players run around the board to collect their paycheck they pay you rent for the temporary use of your property. The more you develop your property the more rent others owe you. This is the power of unearned income.

Learning the difference between earned and unearned income is key to winning Monopoly®. The properties are one kind of capital that generates rents from others that need to use it. Whoever gets slightly more properties at the start of the game, due to the random nature of the dice, will grow their capital faster than those who are only collecting a paycheck. As the game plays out, one player will eventually own enough properties to cause the financial ruin of all other players. That is the goal of the game: acquire as much capital as quickly as possible in order to transfer all the capital owned by other players to yourself. Game over.

In real life, once a controlling amount of the capital is owned by the elite, the only things preventing life from ending like a game of Monopoly® are the laws we established to protect the common good. The laws that prevent a total concentration of capital—a monopoly—help keep freedom possible by preventing any individual from gaining too much power over others.

Freedom is threatened when capital can, and is, used to influence politics. If the elite are in a position to buy laws and economic policy, then what happens to the safeguards for the common good? Some of the most fiercely debated tax laws concern capital gains and inheritance.

Capital Inequality in the United States

In his book, *Capital in the 21st Century*, economist Thomas Piketty documented the distribution of capital in the United States, as of 2010 (Table 7.2), as follows:

- The top 10% have 70% of total capital.
- Within that top 10%, the top 1% own 35%.
- The middle class have 25%.
- The working class have only 5% of the total capital.

Here is an illustration of the capital distribution in the United States today. Imagine a hotel made of one hundred identical single occupant rooms. There will be one hundred people staying there as guests. The hotel represents all the capital resources in North America, with the hundred guests represent the total population of the United States.

The first person gets thirty-five rooms all to himself. He has plenty of room to spread out and relax.

The next nine people also have thirty-five rooms shared between them. Not as much room as the first guy, but they still have almost four rooms each. Combined the first ten people have a total of seventy out of one hundred rooms. The next forty people have twenty-five rooms shared between them. Some of them will have a room to themselves but most will have to fit two people into a single occupant room.

The last fifty people end up having to share the last five rooms—that is ten people in each single occupant room.

In 1980, the pay for a CEO was between thirty to forty times that of the average worker. As of 2011, that number has jumped to three hundred forty-three times that of the average worker. In 2014, the CEO of Walmart earned over one thousand times that of the average worker. This does not seem to bother most of us because we have bought into the belief that somehow CEOs are worth three hundred forty-three times more than those who actually do the work. It is painfully obvious that inequality in the United States is not only massive, but has grown in leaps and bounds over the last century. But is inequality actually a problem?

Poverty in the United States

Levels of Poverty
The definition of poverty is not having sufficient income for basic needs like food, shelter, clothing, and medical care. Stop and think for a moment about what that means. Not having enough money for food, so you are always hungry. Not having a place to stay, so you lack security. Not being able to buy shoes after yours have fallen apart. Having an infection, but being unable to afford antibiotics.

As of 2011, there are 1.46 million families—including 2.8 million children—living in the United States on fewer than two dollars a day, which is fewer than seven hundred dollars a year before any government assistance. In 1996, there were only 636,000 families at this level of poverty. If you have never faced poverty before, try to imagine being responsible for children, a spouse, or aged parents and not having enough to live on. I know this is an uncomfortable thought and it is easier to jump to all the justifications for why someone is impoverished.

Despite the United States being one of the richest countries in the world, it has one of the highest rates of poverty among rich industrial nations. For everyone who has lived to be fifty years old, 42% of those people will have lived in poverty for at least one year of their life. Additionally, 50% of those people will have been near poverty. If we run the numbers out until these people are seventy-five, the numbers climb to 59% in poverty for at least a year and 68% near poverty. Before using the common explanation that poor people are lazy or do not work hard enough, keep in mind that the majority of Americans will experience poverty at some point in their lives—it would be irresponsible to label the majority of Americans as simply "lazy". Looking beyond the why for the moment, let us look at the results of poverty on a person.

Poverty's Effects

Those who remain in poverty for long periods of time experience much higher rates of malnutrition, which is linked to impaired cognitive function, damaged psychological development, depression, and even suicide. Living conditions for the poor are substandard, with high crime rates creating a constant state of stress. Despair is always close at hand for the poor, even before dealing with the way others treat them. The poor are ignored as if they do not exist, are treated condescendingly as though they are children, and, worst of all, they are told it is their own fault for being poor. Just one of the results of living under these conditions is a higher infant mortality rate than the rest of the population.

Why Are People Poor?

Yes, there will always be those individuals content to live off the system who do not need to, but these people are an extreme minority. In my own town, I see people doing backbreaking work picking strawberries in the fields, prematurely aged by the sun. There are others who clean and care for businesses and the homes of the wealthy, doing work that no one else wants to do. These individuals fall into the poor category, but they are clearly not lazy.

American Dream vs. Reality

So why is laziness one of the first explanations people use to explain the problem of poverty? Because we believe if someone has more it is because they have earned it, and that anyone can be just as successful if they try hard enough. The reason this belief has survived in the American mind is because there is some truth to it. There are famous examples of rags to riches stories in the United States that capture our imagination and feed the idea of the American Dream.

The reality of the American dream is that only 4% of children born in the bottom 20% of household income will rise to the top 20% of household income. The class you are born into is the greatest determiner of where you will wind up as an adult. The system is not based on merit; rather, it is based on the privilege of family wealth, education, and the social connections that give access to making it big in America.

The Power of Money

Welfare for the Rich

People complaining about the drain of the poor through the welfare system have not recognized how much the rich benefit from corporate welfare. This should not be surprising, as the upper classes make up the government and create the policies. The well-off receive far more in government handouts than the poor ever have, as I will show you in the coming paragraphs. Corporate handouts come in the form of tax breaks, subsidies, price fixing, government funded research, government funded building projects, and bailouts.

Consider Wal-Mart. In 2014, Fortune Global 500 identified Walmart as the largest company in the world by revenue. In 2013, their revenue was over four hundred seventy-five billion dollars ($475,000,000,000). And yet Wal-

Mart repeatedly received offers from local governments ranging from reduced or no tax rates, free land, and free changes to infrastructure. These are corporate handouts to Wal-Mart that small local businesses would never receive. It has been calculated that Wal-Mart has received over $1.2 billion in corporate welfare, yet they are the largest company in the world.

Or we could look at the largest financial institutions in our country, who have robbed the working class of billions through illegal scams that came to a head in 2008, which resulted in 40% of the world's wealth being wiped out. Almost half of all money in the world vanished. Not only did the officers of these institutions responsible for this devastation see zero jail time, but they received over two hundred billion dollars ($200,000,000,000) in corporate welfare in the form of bailouts.

Even though the National Cancer Institute, a federal laboratory, was instrumental in identifying and testing the use of AZT for the treatment of HIV/AIDS, the private company Burroughs-Wellcome that benefited from the government funded research and labs was able to get an exclusive patent. Burroughs-Wellcome owes no royalties to the government and are not bound by any price restrictions on the sale of the drug.

The 1950s percentage of federal taxes collected from corporations amounted to 28%. By 2010, it was down to only 9%. The poor and middle class are paying a higher proportion of their income in taxes to make up for the decrease from corporations.

The bottom line in answering the question of why people are poor in a country as wealthy as the United States is the unjust economic policies and laws created by the wealthy for the benefit of the wealthy. The policies and laws allow for an ever increasing concentration of wealth and this is justified by the myth of meritocracy. When programs exist for the poor, they are vulnerable to external pressures represented by big money. Access to programs for the poor is often limited, the programs are not well advertised, and the experience can be dehumanizing to the individual by requiring governmental access to the individual's personal information and private living space. Our market is not free. It has rules and regulations for how it works and these rules have implications for how people experience life.

Inequality in Government
If there is doubt that our policies and laws are not controlled by the wealthy, consider what is required to run for political office. It has become a money game. If you do not have millions to spend, you cannot compete. But campaign contributions come with expectations and obligations. Those with huge amounts of money can buy politicians and influence the passing of laws that favor their position. In the 2008 presidential election, the candidates spent $5.3 billion dollars. Often the powerful will donate to both political parties so that they have a foot in the door no matter who wins. This is a serious problem. It effectively locks anyone out of the process that big money does not want to support, which means that our politicians and policies are not representing the people, but big money's interest.

Inequality in Consequence
When laws are broken there is massive inequality in how one is punished based on economic class. We have "Equal Justice Under the Law" engraved on the Supreme Court building in Washington D.C., and Lady Justice is blindfolded. The American experiment is based on the legal system not being a respecter of persons. In 2013, congressman Trey Radel was convicted of cocaine possession and only received probation. In 2014, his record was expunged after completing rehab. There are currently five hundred thousand non-congressmen in prison for nonviolent drug offenses.

The changing laws and systems of our country are leaving broken bodies and casualties behind in its wake. People born into poverty and brokenness with no hope of escape are a liability to the rest of the system. The existence of the poor challenge the mythology of tax breaks for the rich (trickle-down economics) and meritocracy. If the illusion of the system is to continue, the poor and broken need to be labeled defective and removed.

As of 2010, we have almost 2.3 million people imprisoned in the United States. Ours is the largest prison population in the world. The U.S. has only 5% of the world's population, yet has 25% of the world's prison population. If you include jails, almost one out of every hundred adults is incarcerated in North America. Since 1970, there has been a 700% increase in incarcerations, while the population has only increased by 55%.

An extremely disturbing trend is the privatizing of prisons in the United States. In a privatized prison system there is an economic incentive to have inmates. The unemployed, poor, minority men that would normally be a drain to the economic system become a source of revenue for the prison owners. Additionally, these prisons can hire out their inmate population for extremely cheap labor to big business.

"Our prison population, in fact, is now the biggest in the history of human civilization. There are more people in the United States either on parole or in jail today (around 6 million total) than there ever were any time in Stalin's gulags. For what it's worth, there are also more black men in jail right now than there were in slavery at its peak [in the U.S.]" (Taibbi, 2014:xvi).

Our prisons are overcrowded to the point that almost 70% of inmates are warehoused for eighteen or more hours per day in a sixty square foot cell. Think of a space slightly smaller than an 8'x8' room. As many as half of the inmates suffer from some form of mental illness and there is a constant threat of brutality and rape. Prison is designed to be a dehumanizing institution, where a prisoner has no control over most areas of their life. Rather than a time of reform, prisoners learn survival skills that help them become more effective criminals.

The powerless are the ones most often defined as criminals because the powerful, who make the rules, are not going to define their own behavior as criminal. Matt Taibbi, in his book, *Divide: American Injustice in the Age of the Wealth Gap*, contrasts the fate of the poor and the non-consequences of the rich. One example of this contrast is between Tory Marone and the bank HSBC. Tory Marone, a homeless man, is caught sleeping in a park with half a joint in his pocket and is sent to jail. HSBC admits to laundering money on American soil for some of the worst drug cartels and criminal organizations in the world, and pays only a fine equivalent to five weeks of their revenue and must apologize. Matt concludes:

> For aiding and abetting drug cartels suspected in more than twenty thousand murders, groups famous for creating the world's most gruesome torture videos—the Sinaloa Cartel in particular, with its style of high-volume reprisal killings and public chainsawings and disembowelings, makes al-Qaeda look like the Peace Corps—HSBC got to walk. Tory Marone, for smoking their product and passing out on a park bench got sent to jail. This meant the very lowest kind of offender in the illegal drug business, the retail consumer at the very bottom of the drug food chain, had received a far stiffer sentence than the officials at HSBC who were hundreds of millions of dollars deep into the illegal drug business, not for any excusable reason but just to seek profits to pile on top of profits. (Taibbi, 2014:62-63)

We could also explore how "Hands up - don't shoot" and "I can't breathe" have become rallying cries in our day to protest police brutality that clearly run along economic and racial lines. Or we could talk about differences in access to quality medical care or being able to live where there is abundant clean air, water, and safety. The powerless do not have the means to influence political decisions for the location of toxic dumps, air standards in their area, or water regulations.

The values and principles that many believe the United States is meant to embody are yet to be realized. Great progress has been made, but that progress will quickly be reversed as the issues of inequality remain unaddressed. Despite American ideals and efforts, the country will remain a system of domination. This is not how people should experience life, nor how God desires people made in God's image be treated. The Sacred Revolution is the way out. But before we can address the details of the revolution, we need to understand how the domination system is supported.

Religion of the Domination System

A Domination System is a hierarchical culture in which the few benefit at the expense of the many. How does this system remain intact? How does the system keep the majority of the population on the bottom without them overthrowing the few at the top? What causes the fifty people sharing five rooms to remain crammed together, while one guy maintains thirty-five rooms for himself?

In the past, when tyrants openly ruled the world, violence and brutality were commonly used to strike fear into any who dared step out of line. But tyrants could not just slaughter the little people, because hierarchical systems depend on the labor of the masses to keep the system alive. The primary method employed by those at the top, to control the many, is to establish the system of hierarchy as a necessity in the minds of the populace. This is accomplished through propaganda. The means and method of propaganda are what justify the system, and this is the role of religion in any culture.

Religion's Link to Government

In a hierarchical system, authorized violence and religion are the two arms of the-powers-that-be. Authorized violence is the threat that keeps people in line. Religion justifies inequality by claiming divine origins for the way things are. Mystification of how the system works (using needless complexity), keeps those on the bottom from asking questions or challenging the way things are.

The result is that the oppressed fear to challenge the way things are because they risk the wrath of the gods, or the return of chaos, or an even worse fate for themselves. Religious propaganda claims that life is not possible outside of the system. Fear is openly used to control and gain compliance from the masses—not always fear of the system, but fear of what would happen without the system.

Fear of Change

Creating fear is the fastest way to achieve unity and compliance among people. Fearing people who are different from us in some way, we refer to them as "the other." Patriotism is celebrated fear of the other and belief in exceptionalism. Fear of the differences between us and them creates a context in which we dehumanize the other, which justifies the use of violence or oppression against them. Humans do not generally want to hurt other people, but if they can be convinced that the other is somehow less deserving than themselves or is a threat, there is no end to the brutality that humans are capable of.

In a country like the United States that lacks a dictator threatening violence, an additional mode of control is necessary. Here enters the middle class. The middle class has not quite made it to the top, but are doing better than the majority—the lower class. This means that they have a vested interest in maintaining the system and not rocking the boat, even though they also suffer due to economic inequities. The introduction of the middle class has proven to be an effective tool in maintaining class structure. Having "regular" people (those outside the top ten percent) fighting to maintain the system creates the impression that the system is good for everyone instead of just the elites.

The Psychology of Fear

In addition to using the middle class to support a system of domination, psychological tools are employed to convince the people who are suffering that they deserve their lot in life. Multiple scientific and cultural studies have shown that when people are consistently told that they are stupid or lazy, if given the right environment these people will begin to internalize these accusations and believe that they are, indeed, stupid or lazy. We see this in scholastic testing that favors certain cultural backgrounds and social experience, resulting in consistently poor test scores for those outside of the system's favor. The myth of meritocracy fosters the opinion in the mind of the oppressed that, "if anyone can make it, and I am not making it, it must be true that I am lazy or stupid."

The way a problem is defined has the power to maintain the status quo or light a spark that ignites change. If a problem is defined as a personal problem, then the individual turns to internal strategies to cope. For example, if the reason you do not have a job or earn enough money is explained by stating that you are not working hard enough or that you are not smart enough, then upping your work ethic or becoming better educated are examples of using personal resources for change.

Addressing a problem as a personal issue, when the individual cannot change their situation, will lead to coping with the problem either through acceptance or escape. Forms of acceptance or escape that cannot be solved by the individual include: drinking, drugs, suicide, destructive behavior, neurosis, and even physical illness.

On the other hand, if a problem is defined as a social problem, a problem with how the system works, then the individual can employ social strategies to address the problem. For example, the individual can join or start a collective action group or protest. When a social problem is perceived as too big to do anything about, it can also lead to acceptance or escape; however, the individual may retain a healthier sense of self.

Self-Awareness Within a System of Domination
To effectively address a problem, it is important to correctly identify if it is a personal or social problem. If a problem is personal but perceived as social, the individual will find themselves in continuing conflict with the system but unable to effect the needed change within. Conversely, if the problem is social but perceived as personal, then the individual will blame the self without any means to effect the needed change, leading to destructive personal behavior. Domination Systems will define social problems as personal to keep the people they are oppressing from effecting real change to the system, and simultaneously keeping the oppressed dependent on the system.

Even when there are a few individuals that are strong and can resist the lies that they are the problem, these strong individuals tend to fight for their place at the top rather than dismantling the system that was oppressing them. In some respects we suffer from a failure of imagination. We cannot imagine what life would be like if the system changed. It has spoon fed us what we should expect if the system collapsed: a dystopian world of chaos and destruction. If the fifty people who are crammed into five rooms do manage to take for themselves the rooms belonging to those with the most, the system survives. In the end, the fifty recreate the same hierarchical system as before, only now with themselves at the top and others at the bottom.

A Rose by Any Other Name...

At its core, the problem with the Domination System is a religious problem. Changing the leaders or working on new policies are helpful, but as long as the underlying hierarchical way of ordering the world remains in place, then it will still be exploitative and brutal to those on the bottom. To break with hierarchy requires a different religion. A religion that paints a vision for, and justification of: cooperation, interconnectedness, and respect for life.

The common understanding of religion does not seem to take into consideration the role that it plays in justifying how we are organized as a society. We have expanded our understanding of religion so that we can see how it functions beyond personal and private belief. Religion is a collection of stories that together make a claim about how the world should be. When we adopt those stories as our worldview, we are participating in that religion. Any story of the world that someone chooses to follow, whether or not it contains any gods, functions as a religion. That religion defines meaning, goals, and justification for its existence. There is no way to structure a society without it. Sometimes the religion is called by different names (Marxism, Capitalism, Humanism, Patriotism, or even Secularism), but these all function the same as Christianity, Judaism, or Islam. Every religion tells a story about the world and how we should live in it. They define virtue and vice.

The Sacred Revolution is exposing these larger concerns about human life in our world and the role of religion. The God and Jesus found in the Bible focus on these very issues (as we will discuss in the following pages). The religion of Jesus, as found in the Bible, is a direct challenge to the religion of the Domination System. This challenge is the larger picture of religion that is often hidden when the focus is on the individual and their personal and private relationship with God. This personal piety and private religion is another tool of the Domination System. If those running the system can keep us singing "This world is not my home" then we are not going to interfere or concern ourselves with their control and abuse of this world. But this world is our home, and contrary to contemporary Christianity, the creator God is not planning a great escape from creation. God is redeeming all of creation and restructuring life so that it is experienced as abundance and joy by everyone!

What Kind of Revolution?

The Sacred Revolution is not about violently overthrowing the Domination System or the religion that supports it. The Sacred Revolution is about becoming an alternative to the Domination System—an alternative that serves as a critique and indictment of the current system. It is not about being a bandage for the wreckage this world creates. The church is not a volunteer branch of the government to clean up the mess; doing so only enables the destructive behavior and policies to continue. Yes, the Sacred Revolution is about healing those damaged by the Domination System, but it does so by offering them a way out, an opportunity to become part of a new family that knows how to care for its own. The Sacred Revolution's solution to people who are hurting and suffering is not the way of demeaning handouts; it is the way of belonging, meaning, and vocation. The way of shalom.

CHAPTER WORKS CITED

Lauer, Robert H., and Jeanette C. Lauer. *Social Problems and the Quality of Life*. 13th ed. New York: The McGraw-Hill Companies, 2014.

Piketty, Thomas. *Capital in the Twenty-First Century*. Cambridge, MA: The Belknap Press of Harvard University Press, 2014.

Pinker, Steven. *The Better Angels of our Nature: Why Violence Has Declined*. New York: The Penguin Group, 2011.

Taibbi, Matt. *The Divide: American Injustice in the Age of the Wealth Gap*. New York: Spiegel & Grau Trade Paperbacks, 2014.

Part Two

Shalom

"He has told you, O mortal, what is good; and what does the Lord require of you but to do justice, and to love kindness, and to walk humbly with your God?"

- The Prophet Micah

THE SACRED REVOLUTION

One of my children, Sophie, has often been described as a living embodiment of Disney's Pocahontas. With her long straight black hair, bright brown eyes, and slender build, I am not surprised people make the comparison. Sophie is like Pocahontas in more than just her physical appearance. She finds the world a fascinating place, ponders the interconnectedness of all life, and lives unbound by conformity. She loves to question why things are the way they are, such as why money is needed in society, why racism still exists, and why higher education leaves people in suffocating debt. She is definitely my daughter!

Seeing the world through my children's eyes has helped me see how much I have changed. When they were little, I marveled at how innocently they perceived the world. They believed everywhere was a happy, safe place. I remember thinking to myself, "they are going to be disappointed once they discover how the world actually works." But I was not prepared for how I would feel when I witnessed the end of their innocence.

Sophie has been a vegetarian for the last seven years out of a desire to be healthy. Because of that I thought she would be interested in a podcast I had been listening to that discussed the nature of our society's food supply. We sat down on the couch one quiet evening to listen and learned about the domestication of the plants we eat, the restriction in the variety of foods available, and the depletion of nutrients in the soil. We also learned about the use of chemical pesticides, genetically modified foods, and the issues caused by both of these. Not even halfway through the podcast I turned to Sophie and found her crying. At that moment, I realized just how jaded I had become.

It became too easy for me to hear about these issues of environmental destruction and have them affect only me on an intellectual level. I am motivated to work toward achieving sustainability and harmony with creation, but I cannot remember the last time I was moved to tears when thinking about it. Sitting next to Sophie that evening, I realized I no longer felt shocked about how dire things have become. Looking at my seventeen-year-old daughter, I saw the sense of betrayal and hopelessness in her eyes. I could see the panicked questions flitting across her face, "What happens when our food is no longer food? When our water is too toxic to drink? When our air is more poison than oxygen? There is nowhere we can go to get more!" Seeing Sophie's reaction renewed in me the importance of the work of the Sacred Revolution. It also helped Sophie take what we are working for at church and connect it with the world that she and her generation will inherit.

Getting Started

The Sacred Revolution's vision is for shalom, but we live in domination. I have suggested that the path from domination to shalom is accomplished using the top three priorities: gratitude, covenantal faithfulness, and Sacred Communities; but how do we actualize these priorities?

It is time to look to those that have gone before us—those who have recorded their experiences with God and their methods of resisting the Domination Systems found in their day. We must study their failures and their victories, and ultimately their encounters with Jesus. Their writings constitute our Sacred Scripture—the Bible.

I want to start with a passage in the Gospel of Mark where a man asks Jesus what he should do to inherit eternal life. This brief exchange with Jesus touches on many of the key aspects of the Sacred Revolution, giving us a great introduction to Jesus' teaching and his strategy for engaging the Domination System. Read the complete passage from Mark 10:17-31:

As [Jesus] was setting out on a journey, a man ran up and knelt before him, and asked him, "Good Teacher, what must I do to inherit eternal life?" Jesus said to him, "Why do you call me good? No one is good but God alone. You know the commandments: 'You shall not murder; You shall not commit adultery; You shall not steal; You shall not bear false witness; You shall not defraud; Honor your father and mother.'" He said to him, "Teacher, I have kept all these since my youth." Jesus, looking at him, loved him and said, "You lack one thing; go, sell what you own, and give the money to the poor, and you will have treasure in heaven; then come, follow me." When he heard this, he was shocked and went away grieving, for he had many possessions.

Then Jesus looked around and said to his disciples, "How hard it will be for those who have wealth to enter the kingdom of God!" And the disciples were perplexed at these words. But Jesus said to them again, "Children, how hard it is to enter the kingdom of God! It is easier for a camel to go through the eye of a needle than for someone who is rich to enter the kingdom of God." They were greatly astounded and said to one another, "Then who can be saved?" Jesus looked at them and said, "For mortals it is impossible, but not for God; for God all things are possible."

Peter began to say to him, "Look, we have left everything and followed you." Jesus said, "Truly I tell you, there is no one who has left house or brothers or sisters or mother or father or children or fields, for my sake and for the sake of the good news, who will not receive a hundredfold now in this age—houses, brothers and sisters, mothers and children, and fields, with persecutions—and in the age to come eternal life. But many who are first will be last, and the last will be first."

There is a lot packed into this interchange that needs to be examined to correctly understand what is happening and what Jesus means by his challenging words. What follows will be an in-depth exploration of the incredible amount of information contained within each verse of the passage above. I will guide you through this passage a few verses at a time.

Mark 10:17-31

"Why Do You Call Me Good?"

> As [Jesus] was setting out on a journey, a man ran up and knelt before him, and asked him, "Good Teacher, what must I do to inherit eternal life?" Jesus said to him, "Why do you call me good? No one is good but God alone." (Mark 10:17-18)

Why is the first thing out of Jesus' mouth a rejection of being called good, instead of an answer to the important question that was asked? This is a question that many of us would want to ask Jesus if given the opportunity. It is a question about hope in the face of inevitable death—a question that haunts us from the moment we first become aware of death.

The tragedy of life is that we die. The thought of death strikes fear into the hearts and minds of humanity. It is a fear so powerful that most people intentionally avoid thinking about it until they are confronted with mortality. The fear is not of death itself, but of our abandoned responsibilities and the possibility that death is truly the end.

The man's question to Jesus, "What must I do to inherit eternal life," assumes the possibility of eternal life. We will look at what eternal life means a little further on. The man wants to know how Jesus' answer to the question differs from what he has heard from others of his day. Jesus has been creating quite a stir and seems to be challenging traditional understandings and ways of thinking. The man appears to be earnest in his question. He kneels before Jesus and shows Jesus respect by calling him "good teacher." But in Jesus' initial response to the man, Jesus seems annoyed or upset because the man called him "good." What about this statement causes Jesus to respond this way? Answering this question will challenge a common belief about the understandability of the Bible.

The fact that this exchange raises a question should alert us to the fact that there is missing information in the text. The text itself does not contain everything we need to know in order to make sense of the interaction. The Bible is a collection of documents written for cultures fundamentally different from our own and separated by over 2000 years of history. To further the confusion, the books of the Bible are not in chronological order from when they were written and the writings themselves spanned a period of centuries. Each book of the Bible was written for a particular audience, living in a particular culture, at a particular point in the past. Additionally, each author wrote assuming their audience shared knowledge of recent events of their time. The culmination of all these challenges to reading the Bible make comprehending it difficult at best, and helps us understand why so many different interpretations of the Bible exists today.

It is a common belief among Christians that the Bible is written in a way where anyone can pick it up, read it, and instantly understand what it says. This is not true.

Not just anyone can pick up the Bible and read it. For a person to be able to read the Bible or any text for that matter, they must first be educated enough to read. But reading does not automatically imply comprehension and understanding of the text. Not only does a person need to know how to read, but a translation of the Bible must first exist in that person's language. Translation requires someone to learn the ancient languages, histories, and cultures of the biblical text. There is always training and education required for comprehending the Bible, it is a question of exactly how much is actually necessary. Is a primary American high school education sufficient, or does one need advanced training?

The act of reading is a complex process in which symbols are decoded into letters from marks on a page, and groups of letters are assembled into words. Words combine into sentences. Sentences form the basis for meaning. This process requires a cultural context that provides a consistent and shared understanding of each symbol's original meaning. This shared cultural understanding is vital for another aspect of reading: selectivity. A person cannot say everything about anything, which forces us to be selective in both what we write and say. This selectivity inherently produces gaps in our communication process.

Gaps are an unavoidable challenge for all languages. An author will present information to the reader, and the reader must fill in the gaps of what is culturally understood. For example, in the United States when asked, "What do M&Ms do," most would be able to answer, "They melt in your mouth, not in your hands." This is due to understanding a cultural reference to a product most are familiar with. Another example is when Americans hear the phrase, "All rise." This brings to mind the image of a judge entering a courtroom, the sound of rustling clothes as those in attendance rise, and the suspense of learning about the case being tried. There is a lot of information our minds fill in when we read something based on our culture and with a setting we can instantly connect to.

In other parts of the world, people share more information within their cultures than Americans do. The

United States is a melting pot of different cultures, each of which has its own shared information. This situation creates what is known as a low context culture. In a low context culture, communication needs to be more explicit as there is much less shared information between author and reader. When living in a low context culture a person comes to expect that written communication will have the information needed to understand the ideas being communicated. However, when talking about a text from the Bible, we are reading a communication that is coming from a high context culture. This means that the gaps in the biblical text will be even greater than in a typical American communication. An American reader is going to assume that the biblical authors write like American authors, in that all the relevant information needed to understand the text is in the text—but this is not the case.

Understanding written communication requires using the context the author is assuming to fill in the gaps. This is a problem inherent in all languages. The process of filling in the gaps in your native context happens without conscious effort or thought. The challenge of cross-cultural communication stems from the problem of having different shared information than that of the author. If the text is translated into our language, we naively and unconsciously fill in the gaps from our shared cultural context. This leads to misunderstandings of which we are often unaware.

It is commonly said that anyone can read the Bible for themselves and God will lead them to a proper understanding of the passage. This view either assumes the challenge of cross-cultural communication is overcome through divine action, or that the person saying it is unaware that there is a cross-cultural problem to begin with. Reading the Bible without knowing there are cultural differences that need to be kept in mind will lead to misunderstandings.

We should not assume God overcomes the problems of cross-cultural communication for us due to the sincere, yet incompatible, ways individual believers read the same book. If God ensured people understood the message of the Bible correctly, we would not have competing beliefs within the same religion. For those that insist that the Bible was written in such a way that anyone could read and understand it, remember that you are talking about a book that came to us written in ancient Hebrew, some Aramaic, and Koine Greek. That is the book someone would have to pick up and read if it was written in such a way that anyone could understand it.

The Sacred Revolution seeks to practice a respectful reading of our Sacred Scriptures by employing methodologies in our interpretation that honor the people, places, and intentions of the original authors and their audience. A respectful reading requires the use of cultural anthropology, social linguistics, history, ancient languages, and comparative religion to get at the proper context for filling in the gaps. This is a broad enough topic that the next volume in this series is dedicated to the question of how to respectfully read the Bible. For now, we will briefly look at a core cultural perspective of Jesus' world that will help us understand why Jesus rejects being called good.

In Jesus' day, there was a virtue known as honor. Honor was a core value that people lived by, much as America's society is tightly connected with money. Money is not a value but it is a means to the value of autonomy or individualism. The fact that honor, rather than autonomy, is the core value in Jesus' day has significant importance in how we interpret biblical passages. We cannot assume that the biblical author's focus is on individualism when, in fact, it is on honor. To better understand the concept of honor, look at a typical high school where students organize themselves into a pecking order of popularity. Students' popularity provides them access and privilege among their peers that those less popular do not have. This popularity is equivalent to honor. Honor is a socially derived status for an individual within a community. A community will recognize a person as honorable to the degree that the person lives up to the social expectations of that community. Honor is a way of maintaining socially agreed upon norms. Failure to live up to the norms is considered shameful and results in a loss of honor and position in the community's pecking order.

Suppose there was a high school where the students valued large yellow hats above all else. The pecking order for these students would be established by the order of who had the largest hat. The students cannot change hats, as they receive their hats when they are born, and the size and look are determined by what family they are born into. Students inherit their hats, and therefore their social status, from their families.

Students' statuses within the community would control all aspects of their social lives. They would sit at the table by order of their hat sizes. Much like the hats, the primary way someone ended up with their honor status was from their family. What a community chose to honor could change, but the concept still worked the same. They were expected to be friends with people of similar hat size. Who they dated, the sports they were allowed to join, and more were controlled by their yellow hat size. It would be vital that they maintained and protected their hat, which for them is their honor. These large yellow hats that impact every aspect of people's lives are equivalent of the role that honor played in Jesus' world, where there were other social norms that people were expected to follow.

In the United States, we value independence and individualism. Money is a primary way to achieve these things. The more money someone owns, the better their social status. Money is what makes our world go 'round. In Jesus' world, group belonging, especially family belonging, was valued. Honor was the mark of living up to that social norm. Honor is what made the world go 'round in Jesus' day.

The concern for family and the group in Jesus' day led to a keen awareness of how goods were distributed in the community. People at that time thought of community as family. How goods were distributed within the family shaped how they thought about the distribution of goods within the community. In a family there were unequal proportions, but no one would lack what was needed to survive as long as there was something to go around. Imagine a family at the dinner table. The dad probably ate more than young children, but the children would have what they needed.

Unfortunately, there were often not enough goods to go around. This made life especially tough on peasants. When someone in the community gained in some way, the assumption was that it came at the expense of others in the community. This led to people feeling cheated and taking it upon themselves to "balance the books." Therefore, greed was not considered honorable behavior. The primary strategy in life was to maintain social status quo. If a person were to gain more of something, they would either have to distribute their good fortune among the community or work hard to conceal their gain from others. If the person took the latter option and it was discovered, the community would forcibly take steps to correct the imbalance.

One of the primary ways of correcting this balance was to shame the offender. One highly effective way to do this was to call public attention to the person's increase by complimenting them. Verbal sparring and wit were integral parts of the Hebrew culture. Think back to the large yellow hat high school community and imagine someone making their hat a little taller. When the community lines up by hat size, it would be noticed that Johnny's hat is larger. This means that he would need to move up in the line, and someone would then step down. This upsets the social arrangements of who sits with whom, who can be friends with whom, and who can date whom. This cannot be allowed to happen, so Johnny will get called out for his hat's change. The other students might say to Johnny, "Wow Johnny, your hat looks so big!" Johnny now has to either justify the increase in a way the community will accept, which could prove difficult, or successfully convince the others that it has not changed. Otherwise, the community would resize the hat for him, even smaller than before, to shame Johnny for not acting honorably.

With this new insight into how challenges to honor can come in the form of compliments, let's revisit the man's compliment to Jesus, "Good Teacher." This helps explain why Jesus rejects the compliment. It is evident the man viewed Jesus as a threat to the existing social norms regarding who should be in a position to address the question about eternal life. The religious leaders were the ones expected to be in that position, not some random carpenter from the backwoods town of Nazareth. The dynamics of seeing the compliment as a challenge changes the context of the interaction between the man and Jesus. The man is trying to restore balance to the way things were before Jesus started changing things. As we will see in the rest of this passage, the man has a vested interest in keeping things as they have been. Jesus' response to being called "good teacher" is not an act of humility, but rather a brilliant deflection of a shaming technique designed to put Jesus in his place.

This was a long-winded answer to the question of why Jesus does not accept the compliment. The lengthy answer was necessary for us to uncover what is assumed in the text and by the people of Jesus' time, but we are unaware of. Our ignorance of such matters leads to ingenious interpretations, such as claiming that this is an example of Jesus' humility, but that interpretation is wrong. A respectful reading of our Sacred Scriptures necessitates that we let go of the naive view that the Bible is readily understandable and reevaluate our previously held beliefs about what the Bible teaches. This is an example of how we are leaving Christianity to follow Jesus. It is time to see where following Jesus will lead us.

Given that Jesus has successfully dealt with the challenge to his honor, let's look at how he answers the man's question, "What must I do to inherit eternal life?"

"You Know the Commandments"

> [Jesus replies to the man:] You know the commandments: "You shall not murder; You shall not commit adultery; You shall not steal; You shall not bear false witness; You shall not defraud; Honor your father and mother." (Mark 10:19)

The man is asking what he needs to do to inherit eternal life, and Jesus says, "You know the commandments." Why is Jesus' response so entirely different from the response we so often hear from many modern-day Evangelical pastors, "If you died tonight, do you know for certain that you would go to heaven?" The pastor will often then continue by saying, "if you are unsure, then bow your head and repeat the sinner's prayer with me now." Nothing about commandments. What has happened?

The way the question is phrased and answered, reveals how contemporary Christianity understands the concept of salvation. According to the contemporary view, salvation means that you go to heaven rather than hell. The solution to making sure you go to heaven is to say the sinner's prayer, sometimes referred to simply as accepting Jesus as your personal Lord and Savior. The contemporary Christian view makes salvation a personal, private, and intellectual concern that involves escape from the physical world (going to heaven) and escape from the physical body (the soul is set free from the body).

But again, Jesus' response to the man's question about how to inherit eternal life is not expressed in terms of saying a prayer or believing the right things about God. Why is Jesus' response so different from the contemporary Christian response? We get a clue when we look at how we have rephrased the question: how to go to heaven when you die versus how to inherit eternal life. This might not sound so different at first glance, but there is a big difference between these two questions, and Jesus' response helps us to understand what that is. You see, the concept of eternal life in the Bible is not about going to heaven when you die, as strange as that may sound to you.

Part of the reason for the confusion in our contemporary Christian context is because there is a dichotomy we have created between concepts of grace and law. It is common to believe that the Old Testament was all about demanding laws that one had to keep, and if you did not keep them all properly, then you were going to be condemned to Hell. Additionally, it is believed that Jesus came to rescue us from needing to be saved through the law, and this new way is by grace. In this view, rather than keeping the law, one just needs to acknowledge Jesus' saving work on our behalf. So the idea that Jesus is now saying "keep the commandments" seems to be entirely contrary to what we would expect in our current context. It just does not fit the contemporary Christian view of salvation.

We need a better understanding of the Old Testament "law" to make sense of what Jesus is saying and why. To begin with, our English word "law" has a narrower range of meaning than what exists in both the Hebrew and Greek words used in the Bible. Law in a biblical sense also carries with it the idea of a path or way of life. This way of life is codified in a covenant. We need to look at a brief overview of Israel's history to have a better understanding of how covenant functions and what its purpose is.

The History of the Covenant

Abraham is the father, the first patriarch, of Israel. He was called out of the city Ur in Mesopotamia, the birthplace of civilization for the world. Abraham left the city to take on a new way of life. He was to become a nomadic wanderer—a herdsman in the faraway land of Canaan. Because of a drought, the decedents of Abraham settled in Egypt, a great empire of the ancient world. The Israelites were in Egypt for over four hundred years, and Abraham's descendants wound up as slaves. They were eventually freed from Egypt in the Exodus. They come out of the empire of Egypt and again into an alternative way of life: the way of covenant over the way of empire. The Exodus is the foundational story of salvation in the Old Testament.

There are two key events that happen in the Exodus. First, while the slaves were still in Egypt, there was the event of the Ten Plagues. The plagues were as much for Israel as they were against Egypt. In the world of Pharaoh, his word was law and he was seen as the ultimate leader—a god on Earth. The plagues systematically deconstructed all the claims that Pharaoh made. The way of hierarchy, maintained by force, was the way the world worked and the only life that generation of Israelites had ever known. One of the hardest things for them, or anyone, was to envision a life outside of what they currently knew.

The world the Israelites had in Egypt was one where order was maintained by brutal force, with the masses serving the elite out of gratitude for the protection that Pharaoh gave. The gods had decreed that the way of Pharaoh was law. If enslaved Israel was rescued from Egypt and just plopped down in the new home God was promising them, they would have only recreated Egypt but with themselves on top and somebody else on the bottom. It was the only way of life they had known for four hundred years. As much as they may have suffered under the system, the existence and grandeur of Egypt was evidence that Pharaoh's way was right. Freed slaves were not looking for a new system, they wanted a new position within the existing system. Before they could be liberated bodily from Egypt, they also had to be liberated mentally. They had to be freed from this Pharaonic vision how life worked in order to envision a new, successful way of life.

The second key event of Exodus happened after the Exodus and before Israel entered the Promised Land. The Ten Plagues deconstructed the vision of life ordered according to hierarchy, and so Israel needed to have a vision for life reconstructed. Just as there were ten plagues to deconstruct, God gave ten words to reconstruct. In English we often refer to them as the Ten Commandments, but in Hebrew it is actually the Ten Words. This is the core covenant of Israel with God. The Ten Words are not functioning as a law that somebody has to keep in order to earn salvation—they are the result of salvation. The people were being saved from the way of Pharaoh and brought to the way of covenant.

Covenant is defining a relationship between God and the people, and the people with each other. It is defining an alternative way of life to the way Israel was experiencing under Pharaoh. In fact, when they finally reached the Promised Land, Israel existed as a people without a centralized government or hierarchy for over two hundred fifty years. That is longer than the United States has been a country. Israel, as a collection of tribes, were bound together by this vision of covenant for how they structured and organized life. Think of the covenant more like a constitution than a law. A constitution is not law, it is defining what kind of people we desire to be. Then you have all sorts of case law that works out how to enact what is trying to be accomplished with the constitution. So the covenant functions like a constitution as it defines what kind of people Israel is supposed to be.

When viewing this idea of salvation from an Old Testament perspective, it is not about the idea of how we get to heaven when we die. In fact, in the Old Testament there is little discussion about an afterlife; rather, it focuses on what is needed to restructure life in the present so that people experience life to its fullness. To restructure life in such a way as to bring abundance and joy to everyone. To restructure life so that no one goes without so that others can have excess.

It is a restructuring of society in a radical way that is meant to be entirely different from the vision of empire, in which there are a few who benefit at the expense of the many. Egypt, with its pyramids, becomes a primary example of what that way of life looks like. Later, Babylon will become another one of the paradigmatic examples of empire in Israel's history.

Israel existed for a great deal of time as a collection of tribes that were bound together by covenant. Then, a crisis: a very powerful people called the Philistines moved into town. Coinciding with the arrival of the Philistines, there was a crisis of religious leadership within Israel. These two events led the people of Israel to demand a ruler like their pagan neighbors, becoming a people bound by covenant transition to having a king. This led to a new way of life that proved to be disastrous for Israel.

The first king did not do a very good job, but the second king, David, united the tribes and conquered the remaining peoples in the Promised Land. He took Jerusalem for himself and called it the City of David, beginning the process of transitioning Israel from a collection of tribes into a nation-state.

David's son and the third king, Solomon, built Israel into a strong nation, constructing the Temple and establishing the palace. With Solomon, Israel gained a fully functioning kingship nation-state.

By the time Solomon died and his son was about to take over, the people were very upset about the harsh treatment they had received under Solomon. In order to build the Temple and the palace, he had conscripted his own people into forced labor and hired what they considered pagan workers to come in and build the Temple.

Israel essentially returned to the structure of Egypt and into a situation of slavery. When Solomon's son was about to take over, a delegation came to him and said, "Are you going to relent from the harsh practices of your father?" The son said, "If you thought my father's practices were harsh, my little finger is thicker than his whole waist." The delegation basically responded, "Well, forget it. We don't want anything to do with you."

There was a split. The northern tribes broke away from the southern tribes and divided into two different kingdoms. There was so much corruption in both kingdoms that the very survival of Israel was at stake.

A mighty power came out of Mesopotamia—the Assyrians—and conquered the northern tribes of Israel. Those northern tribes were never heard from again. Assyria's practice, when they came in and conquered a land, was to take the people and split them up. They would remove small groups and take them to different countries and provinces. This practice prevented the conquered people from maintaining the identity of their way of life.

Around two hundred years later the southern kingdom was ultimately conquered by the Babylonians. Fortunately, they did not disperse the conquered people all over; Babylon took the best and the brightest from Israel and brought them to Babylon.

Babylon was eventually conquered by the Persians. At that point the Israelites were allowed to return to their homeland to rebuild the temple and attempt to reestablish their way of life. By using client kings from the conquered leaders—allowing a level of freedom for the price of loyalty—Persia would have greater control over the people. Israel was back in her homeland, but was still occupied. Soon it would be Alexander the Great and his successors, followed by Pompey, who conquered Israel for Rome. Which brings us to the New Testament.

This is a brief history of Israel from Abraham to Jesus to help you to see an interesting pattern. It is a pattern of God calling people out of lives defined by empire. God calls Abraham's family out of Mesopotamia and the nation of Israel out of Egypt, each time to lead them to an alternative way of life where they would be defined by a covenant rather than by a domination model where a few control the many. Israel's return to life defined by empire and confining God to a temple was a near fatal move.

Not all of the biblical writers felt the same way. There are two main views expressed in the Bible. One is supportive of the kings, where Solomon is praised as the pentacle of Israel's glory and called the "wisest of the wise." The second has the prophets denouncing the kings and the aristocracy of the time and saying, "Look, you are only experiencing your wealth and power on the backs of the poor. This is wrong." The basis for the prophetic critique of empire and the aristocracy is the covenant.

The challenge is that both the way of covenant defined by the prophets and the way of kings defined by the aristocracy are supported by claiming that God ordained them. Jesus is a prophet.

That God would have so much to say at a political level is a new idea to many people who have been told not to mix religion and politics. Understanding the Sacred Revolution requires a reorientation to the Bible and its concerns. To demonstrate this, I would like to look at three key concepts of the Bible that show God's regard for how life is structured and ordered in the here and now. These three topics are: the image of God, the Sabbath, and the resurrection.

The Image of God

The concept of the image of God did not originate in the Bible. In fact, in the ancient near East there are people who were considered to be the image of God. These were the kings or the pharaohs. They were believed to be God's representatives on earth. Because of their exalted status, people were expected to submit to their authority. Just imagine what people of that day must have thought when they heard or read that the sacred writings of the Hebrews declared that all people were, in fact, made in the image of God!

> So God created humankind in his image, in the image of God he created them; male and female he created them. (Genesis 1:27)

Can you see what kind of revolutionary statement this was? Not only were all men made in the image of God, but women, too. If everyone is made in the image of God, then this destroys the whole class, hierarchical structure of the ancient world. And the modern world, for that matter. If everyone is made in the image of God, then any system where a few benefit at the expense of the many is unacceptable. Just try to imagine the modern-day repercussions if Christians took this seriously.

The Sabbath

Next, let's briefly consider the concept of Sabbath. You might find it interesting to note that the Sabbath was not given for worship in the Bible. The Sabbath was first and foremost an economic practice.

> Remember the sabbath day, and keep it holy. Six days you shall labor and do all your work. But the seventh day is a sabbath to the Lord your God; you shall not do any work—you, your son or your daughter, your male or female slave, your livestock, or the alien resident in your towns. For in six days the Lord made heaven and earth, the sea, and all that is in them, but rested the

seventh day; therefore the Lord blessed the sabbath day and consecrated it. (Exodus 20:8-11)

On the Sabbath people were commanded to disengage from the whole economic apparatus. Everyone was to have rest. This included the servants, as no one could have people wait on them while they rested. Not only people, but even the animals themselves were commanded to rest. This challenges the whole people-as-a-machine idea and the 24x7 cycle. People were not created to be cogs in the wheel. Sabbath was a weekly event that set everyone as equal, challenging the mode of constant acquisition and replacing it with learning enoughness. Every seventh year there was also what was called a "yearly Sabbath."

> The Lord spoke to Moses on Mount Sinai, saying: Speak to the people of Israel and say to them: When you enter the land that I am giving you, the land shall observe a sabbath for the Lord. Six years you shall sow your field, and six years you shall prune your vineyard, and gather in their yield; but in the seventh year there shall be a sabbath of complete rest for the land, a sabbath for the Lord: you shall not sow your field or prune your vineyard. You shall not reap the aftergrowth of your harvest or gather the grapes of your unpruned vine: it shall be a year of complete rest for the land.
> (Leviticus 25:1-5)

At this point the land is also to have rest in which it is not to be farmed. What is produced during the seventh year can be used, but no one is supposed to work the land. In addition, all are released from their debts at the same time every seventh year.

> Every seventh year you shall grant a remission of debts. And this is the manner of the remission: every creditor

shall remit the claim that is held against a neighbor, not exacting it of a neighbor who is a member of the community, because the Lord's remission has been proclaimed. (Deuteronomy 15:1-2)

So in addition to the economic break in the weekly Sabbath, you also have the problem of ongoing indebtedness tackled with this yearly Sabbath. It also protects the land from overuse by people in the same way people and animals are protected from overuse in the weekly Sabbath.

Then we have what is called the "Jubilee," which comes at the conclusion of a series of seven cycles of this seven-year Sabbath in the 50th year. The jubilee was to be a grand celebration in which all of the other Sabbath requirements would come together. Additionally, anybody who found themselves in a position where they had to sell their land prior to the Jubilee would receive their family land back. So the problem of ongoing indebtedness is dealt with and also the problem of ongoing landlessness. Leviticus 25:8-10, 23-28 details the process.

These are controls that are put in place for the people of God to protect even those who are most at risk in society, such as widows and orphans. These laws are reflecting a concern for the vision: that all people are made in the image of God and life can be experienced to the fullest by everyone, not just a select few.

Note that the justification that the land could not be sold in perpetuity was because they understood that everything belongs to God (Leviticus 25:23). We do not actually own, in a real sense, anything. We are only here for a short time, and everything we receive we receive as a gift; therefore, we are not in a position to have actual, permanent control over anything.

Think about what kind of community is shaped by these Sabbath practices. There is a radical equalizing of everyone on the weekly Sabbath where all are given rest. There is prevention of perpetual indebtedness by canceling debts every seven years. Perpetual landlessness is cancelled out by the return of the land every fifty years. There are real concerns, and safety nets for those who are most at risk within this type of a community. In fact, other regulations prevented things like harvesting all of the food off of the land so that those who are in need could find food. Also employers are warranted to pay their workers in a timely manner or else the workers might cry out and God would hear their cry, and the employers would find themselves in God's judgment.

These are not the commands of a God who is only concerned about private, personal spirituality and the escape from creation to heaven. These are the commands of a God who is deeply concerned about life and its ability to be enjoyed by all. His commands are focused on how to bring about life being experienced to the fullest, and the protection of those who are most at risk within the community.

These two concepts then, the image of God in all people and the commands regarding the Sabbath, present a world that is in stark contrast to our modern-day way of living. Not because these are antiquated ways of existing, but because they are a radically different way of perceiving who people are, and what our relationship to God and creation should be.

The Resurrection

Foundational to faith in Jesus is the resurrection. The resurrection of Jesus stands as God's vindication that Jesus is, in fact, God's Messiah and the fullest revelation of God's true nature. But this was not some metaphorical way of explaining the spirit of Jesus living on within our memory, or that Jesus' soul had escaped his body and is now in heaven. No, all the Gospel accounts make a point of the empty tomb. Jesus was raised to life physically. To make sure the disciples did not misunderstand what had happened to him, Jesus invited them to touch him to prove that he was not a ghost.

The resurrection is not about surviving death, it is about the reversal of death. This is the hope that is presented to us. As followers of Jesus, we are told that we will also participate in the final resurrection of all the faithful. Jesus' resurrection is the promise that the future resurrection is not only possible, but is the way that God will finally restore creation to the way it was always meant to be.

Resurrection creates two simple affirmations: first, the body is good. It is very easy in some faith traditions to have a negative view of the physical body or to equate it with the idea of sinfulness, something to deny, or something we ultimately escape from at death. Resurrection turns that thinking on its head. Second, the created order is good. The physical world is not seen as something that is evil or something to escape because resurrection happens in this world, not somewhere else.

The apostle Paul tells us that all of creation is waiting for our transformation, because at that time creation itself will be released from its bondage to decay. Every time we pray the Lord's Prayer, "Your kingdom come, your will be done, on earth as it is in heaven," we anticipate that day. In the book of Revelation's conclusion, we learn that God will once again dwell with people here on earth, and there will be no more tears.

You see, the ultimate goal of the Sacred Revolution is not the escape from physical creation to some disembodied spiritual existence in heaven; rather, it is the redemption of all of creation, including people. That is why what we do now matters. There is continuity between the here and now and the age of the resurrection. This is why God is so concerned about life and how we live it. This life is not just some training ground for some entirely different kind of existence—this life is what it is all about! What we live and work for in this world matters because this is not all getting scraped. It will be redeemed and all that is good, and just, and right will last.

All three of these biblical concepts, then, should reorientate us as to what the Sacred Revolution is all about. The elevation of all people as made in the Image of God, challenging all systems of hierarchy; the radical economic and equalizing aspects of the Sabbath commands; and the promise of resurrection, all point to a God that is very "this world" focused. It is not all about you or me, it is not about personal, private faith, it is about all of life and how we are to live together in a way that brings about abundance and wholeness for everyone: shalom.

Shalom is about life in right relationship and well-being. When we are in right relationship with other people and creation, we are in right relationship with God. Conversely, we cannot be in right relationship with God if we are not in right relationship with others and creation.

When people are in right relationship with each other, it will be marked with integrity, accountability, and concern. When people are in right relationship to creation, economic and infrastructure policies will be characterized by sustainability and cooperation. The focus on relationship reveals an understanding that everything is interconnected.

To teach and support the shalom way of life requires structures to support it, and this is where covenant comes in. The covenant provides the framework through which we can develop policies and practices that help us be a people that are shaped and formed into shalom people—God's people.

The test for shalom is the well-being of those that are most at risk in a society—those that have no voice or power, and could be easily overlooked. The Bible uses the trio of the widows, orphans, and aliens. In other places, the Bible also lifts up the concern for the land as well.

At the end of the day, shalom must be experienced by all or else it is a false peace. Shalom requires the end of oppression, violence, and the just distribution of resources;

therefore, shalom can be equated with justice. But if shalom will be experienced by all, the type of justice will focus on restoration and reconciliation over punishment.

The Priority of Covenantal Faithfulness

The way of shalom is, in part, defined and supported by the covenant. This topic will require a volume in this series all to itself, but here is a brief overview. As mentioned before, this covenant is more commonly known as the Ten Commandments in English, and in Hebrew as the Ten Words. They come to us not as harsh law, but as words of life. God rescued his people from a brutal life of oppression under Pharaoh. All empires live in fear that there is not enough to sustain their rule, so they strive to produce more food, taller walls, more efficient weapons, all while using their subjects like machines. Empires take by using violence, and they rule by the fear of exclusion or death. God saved his people from Pharaoh physically and mentally.

We have to learn that the way of Pharaoh is false; that the way of Pharaoh is not the way the world works. God systematically deconstructs the false claims of Pharaoh with the ten plagues. God's people are saved from the way of Pharaoh and brought through the covenant to a new way of understanding the world. They are brought to a new way of life—life as it was intended to be. God's people were not saved by the covenant, they were saved to it. The covenant is what it looks like to be in shalom. The way of the covenant is not an easy one in a world determined to go in a different direction, but the prophet Jeremiah promised us that God would make the covenant new and that it would be written in our very being. Here is a paraphrased version of the covenant found in Exodus 20:1-17 with a brief explanation:

1. Serve no other gods before YHWH.

   Our sole allegiance is to God alone. All other claims of authority are suspect and subject to our loyalty to God.

2. Do not use idols.

   It matters how we worship God. We are not to use the ways of the world that box God in and try to control God for our own purposes. There is only one image of God in the Bible and that is people. People were created in the image of God. We reduce what it means to be human when we worship God incorrectly.

3. Do not misuse the name of YHWH.

   We blaspheme God when we think we can stamp God's name on our project or nation or war, using God to justify our domination and violence of others; we believe we can use people as things or as acceptable losses in our endeavors for wealth or security or toys.

4. Remember the Sabbath, to keep it holy.

   It is in the remembering and keeping of the Sabbath that the whole 24/7 production cycle is broken and we learn to trust God for provision and enjoy the life we have been given. The Sabbath is a statement about economics and justice before it says anything about worship.

5. Honor your father and mother.

6. Do not kill.

7. Do not commit adultery.

8. Do not steal.

9. Do not bear false witness against your neighbor.

   The various statements about how we are to treat our neighbor show us that all people are to be respected. We are not free to use people for our own ends.

10. Do not covet.

The first word and the last word of the covenant work like bookends. It is our loyalty and allegiance to God that provides the reason for keeping the covenant, and it is in our coveting something that does not belong to us that we break the covenant.

The covenant makes possible the life of community we all desire. Here we begin to see what love of God and love of neighbor looks like. God has shown faithfulness to us, in that Jesus was willing to endure death for the sake of our redemption. In his faithfulness, we can begin to see the depth of our creator's love for us. In light of the resurrection of Jesus, we learn we can trust God and that if we follow the shalom way of life, God is able to bring us to that promised day. With this confidence, we can lay down our fear. Our neighbor is no longer a competitor for our security, rather now our neighbor is a fellow creature made in the image of God, to whom we can, and must, show love. In fact, our response to our neighbor is in a very real sense our response to God. Consider what John tells us:

> Those who say, "I love God", and hate their brothers or sisters, are liars; for those who do not love a brother or sister whom they have seen, cannot love God whom they have not seen. The commandment we have from him is this: those who love God must love their brothers and sisters also. (1 John 4:20-21)

We cannot be indifferent to our neighbor and think that we are following Jesus. As disciples of Jesus, we look forward to the restoration of the earth when shalom is established and justice and mercy rule the day. At that time people will be devoted to their creator and learn to love God with all their might and their neighbor as themselves. However, it is not enough to long for that day, as we are commissioned to do God's will right here and now, on earth as it is in heaven. To that end, we are to become a community of disciples who are learning together how to live. We are not just offering an idea to a confused and hurting world; rather, we are becoming a tangible example of what it looks like when people live together in faithfulness to their God.

We return again to Jesus' response to the man's question about what one must do to inherit eternal life. Jesus did not tell him to say a prayer so that when he died he would go to heaven. Jesus reminded the man about the covenant. Jesus' answer is about participating in the covenant—participating in the restructuring of the present to bring about shalom for all.

Eternal life—salvation—is so much more than an individual's personal salvation. Salvation is the redemption of creation where all of life is restored to the way it was always intended to be by our Creator. Which means how we live matters. Keeping the commandments is not about a life of rules, it is about a life lived in covenant. It is a covenant that recognizes our interdependence and need to care for one another to have the life that God desires for us. It makes sense that our entering into the covenant and participating in its way of life is how we enter into eternal life. Righteousness means life in right relationship, and that right relationship is defined in the covenant.

Continuing Mark 10:17-31

"Sell What You Own"

> [The man] said to him, "Teacher, I have kept all these since my youth." Jesus, looking at him, loved him and said, "You lack one thing; go, sell what you own, and give the money to the poor, and you will have treasure in heaven; then come, follow me." (Mark 10:20-21)

The man states that he has done what Jesus said to do since he was a child. Why does he do that? Why not just thank Jesus after he gets his answer, especially if it outlines something he is already doing? It feels like the man is expecting something more, and so he engages Jesus further.

Jesus senses that the man is not satisfied. He looks at the man, and the Bible says that Jesus loved him. As we have seen, the man comes to Jesus with a challenge, and now the man pushes Jesus for more. Jesus is going to address the core of the issue, which will challenge the man in a serious way, but it is out of love that Jesus does so.

Sell what you own, and give the money to the poor.

We have moved beyond simply saying the sinner's prayer at this point. Could you imagine the response a modern pastor would get if he told someone that they had to sell everything to be saved? Even if Jesus himself were here and asked you to sell it all, could you? Why is Jesus suggesting that the man does this? Is this something that all followers of Jesus are expected to do?

It is important to note that the commands that Jesus lists are the ones dealing with how we are to treat our brothers and sisters:

> You shall not murder; You shall not commit adultery; You shall not steal; You shall not bear false witness; You shall not defraud; Honor your father and mother. (Mark 10:19)

The astute reader will have noticed that one of the commandments has changed. The command to not covet is replaced with, "you shall not defraud." In Matthew's version of this account this is added: "you shall love your neighbor as yourself." Matthew's addition forms an excellent summary of the commands about caring for your neighbors, but what is the point of Mark's, "you shall not defraud"? Defrauding others would not be keeping with caring for your neighbors, and as we will see, it speaks directly to the issue Jesus uncovered with his statement to the man.

It is important to note that all of the commands listed are the ones directed to one's neighbor. All of the commands related to God are absent. This gives us a clue about what is coming. There is an issue that is either not being addressed by the man, or an issue that the man is unaware of.

> When [the man] heard this, he was shocked and went away grieving, for he had many possessions.
> (Mark 10:22)

The man left. The cost of following Jesus was too great. Jesus loved the man, but that did not prevent him from saying what needed to be said. Following Jesus is more than holding certain beliefs or saying the sinner's prayer. It is about a way of life. How we live matters. But we still need to understand why Jesus said this to the man, and if selling everything is required of all his followers.

Recall when I was explaining about honor and the peasant concern for how goods are distributed. In cultural anthropology terms, the people of Jesus' time held to a concept of limited good. Limited good is a view of the world in which all things are limited and what there is has already been divided up. Imagine a dinner party where you, six of our friends, and I are gathered and we are going to have pie. The pie is limited in that there is only one pie, and the pie is divided into eight pieces. The only way for someone to have more pie is to take it from someone else at the party. Because we are all friends, to take from someone would be considered deviant behavior. People who hold to a limited good view of the world take this same idea as we see with the pie and apply it to all of life. It is easy to see how it applies to things like land, but they apply it to intangible items like honor and love as well. When you live in a limited good world, honorable behavior is not to amass as much as you can—this is viewed as stealing. The honorable way to live in a limited good world is to maintain the status quo. Because American culture does not recognize limited good as a reality, we have a hard time grasping a world in which greed is not okay. Understanding this perspective of the world will help explain why greed is so thoroughly condemned in our Bible.

Many will argue that we do not live in a limited world, but is that true? Are we not limited to the resources we have on our planet? Is there somewhere we can find more fresh water after we ruin all the water we have? How about our land and air? What has happened is that we have hidden the cost for our abundance. In our global world we can destroy the environment of other countries and take advantage of the poor for cheap labor or slave labor to create our inexpensive goods. Just because we cannot see it, does not mean we are not taking from others in order to maintain our lives of relative luxury. Our world IS a closed system. There IS only so much of everything. If we have an abundance, there WILL be those that go without, whether we see them or not.

How does this play out in Jesus' statement to the man? Jesus' listing of the commands that deal with how we treat our neighbor was specifically because the man had many possessions. When the man said that he had kept these commands, Jesus' response was essentially, "Oh really, then how is it that you have so much? If you want to truly keep those commands to love your neighbor as yourself you will need to sell those many possessions and distribute them to your neighbors that have been going without." The young man walks away, unable to part with his possessions.

"Easier for a Camel to Go Through the Eye of a Needle"

Then Jesus looked around and said to his disciples, "How hard it will be for those who have wealth to enter the kingdom of God!" And the disciples were perplexed at these words. But Jesus said to them again, "Children, how hard it is to enter the kingdom of God! It is easier for a camel to go through the eye of a needle than for someone who is rich to enter the kingdom of God." (Mark 10:23-25)

What is Jesus doing? Is he trying to turn away the rich and have all of us sell everything we have? No. But he is telling us that we have to get this "love your neighbor" thing right or we are not going to fit into the life to come. In making this claim, Jesus introduced two new concepts here that need some explanation: wealth and kingdom.

Wealth is a measure of experience over a measure of assets. Wealth is about freedom and opportunities that others do not have. For example, let's say everyone I know made one hundred thousand dollars per year, but I made one million per year. My experience of life is going to be very different from theirs. I am going to have access to things they do not have access to, such as nice gated communities, nicer cars, and being able to send my kids to nicer schools. What happens if we all make one million dollars per year? My experience of greater opportunities and access to nicer things does not exist any longer. There is no experience of wealth if we are all making the same, even though we are all making one million per year. The reason for this is because there is no inequality. The concept, the very experience of wealth, requires that inequality exists in order for someone to have the experience of wealth.

The term "Kingdom" is in the language of Jesus' day. It is making a contrast between the kingdoms of Egypt, Babylon, or Rome—basically any super power ruling as a Domination System—and the way of God. By calling the way of God a Kingdom, it alerts us to what sphere of life is being addressed. Jesus is not talking about a new interior, private belief system, but rather that the Kingdom of God is an alternative way of structuring how life is lived in the public, political sphere. The Kingdom of God is another way of expressing shalom. The feeling we have that the world should be different and that things are not the way they are supposed to be is our internal longing for life to be ordered according to shalom, the Kingdom of God, and to beauty. The Kingdom of God refers to a time in the future when God's will is being practiced, and all of creation has been redeemed. Redemption has already begun with Jesus and is being continued by his followers.

Kingdom is not a term we use to describe our social structure anymore. Perhaps a better term might be "republic" or "nation state." The problem with all these terms is that when we are talking about God's alternative, we imagine God's Kingdom, Republic, or Nation State as essentially the same kind of structure, but with the right people in power and correct policies in place. This is not an accurate image of God's alternative. God's way is an entirely different way of structuring life. The more traditional term for this is the way of shalom. That helps us imagine more clearly what is meant by the Kingdom of God, so that is the phrase I will commonly use throughout this book. But when you see kingdom of God used in the scripture quotations, know that it means shalom.

Now that we have looked at the meaning of wealth and the kingdom, why does Jesus say that the wealthy will have a harder time getting into the kingdom than a camel would have to go through the eye of a needle?

Here is the issue with wealth and the Kingdom of God. To experience wealth means that there is inequality within the system. It means that some are experiencing more advantage and freedom than others. But why is this wrong? We live in a culture that teaches us that anyone can make it if they just try hard enough. If that is true, then all those who are lacking their basic needs in this country are lazy and do not work hard enough. But when I look around some of the hardest working people, people breaking their backs to pick our food, clean our toilets, and maintain our yards will never make it. Are they lazy? I work two jobs just to make ends meet and they make me look lazy in comparison. The reality is that in our system everyone cannot make it. Our system depends on the majority not making it and is structured to keep it that way. Only those from privilege can afford to get the education and opportunities to make it in our culture. There will be a few of the underclass who are allowed through with scholarships and the like, to keep the illusion in place that anyone can make it if they try hard enough.

I am not saying that there should not be any distinctions between people or that someone should not be rewarded for hard work. What needs to be reconsidered is how someone is rewarded and what efforts should be regarded as worthy of recognition. If the actions we reward and the means of the reward mean that billions of people go without their basic needs for survival while a few live in unbelievable luxury, then something is terribly wrong and the system has become inhumane. A recent article came out that documented that the eighty-five people at the top end of our economic system have as much wealth and resources as the bottom half of the world's population combined. Just eighty-five people have as much between them as 3.5 billion people have between them. Does that concern you? What might that mean regarding freedom when so few control so much? Those at the top have the resources to protect and maintain their advantage.

Another problematic aspect of wealth is that it is a tool to escape from our interconnectedness in an attempt to be independent and autonomous. One of the reasons that God calls us to love our neighbor is that we all need each other and are affected by each other. When we are interconnected, we are more aware of our actions and their impact on those we are connected with. When we strive to be free of our responsibility to our neighbor by becoming independently wealthy, we are no longer accountable for our actions.

The world's definition of wealth is incompatible with the Kingdom of God in which there will be no more tears or sorrow, no more poor, and no more starving. Not because we will no longer be capable of crying or needing food, but because we will have learned to care for one another and share with each other. This is why it is like a camel trying to get through the eye of the needle—there is no room for the mentality of inequality in the Kingdom of God. We are called to recognize our interdependence with our neighbor now in preparation for life in the Kingdom. If we do not desire the covenant way of life now, we are not going to want to live that way for eternity.

As long as we are caught up in the game of inequality, and the need to have an experience of having more than someone else, we are not going to enter into the kingdom. Not because we are unable to, but because we are not going to want to.

If the Kingdom of God is about people being related to each other as brothers and sisters—and caring for each other as brothers and sisters—then the Kingdom of God, the way of shalom, is not going to appeal to us if we are hung up on how we get our fair share.

The reason money makes the world go 'round for us in America is because it gives us freedom and autonomy. But what it gives us freedom from is each other. Ultimately, what we have done within our current system is to create the illusion of the individual and that autonomy is possible. We talk about people who are self-made, and that they have risen to the heights of their existence through their own efforts. But it is all an illusion because we are still all totally interdependent on each other.

What we have done is bought into the idea that we are no longer face-to-face accountable to each other for our actions. We have put all of our resources into the shared pool of the government, which then provides an anonymous infrastructure that we are not accountable to.

I could be the richest rock star in the world making billions of dollars, but at the end of the day I am still dependent on people buying my music and coming to my shows. I am dependent on the system that has a common currency. I am dependent on a whole network of banks, and people having jobs at businesses that pay them in that common currency. And people can get there because roads, street signs, cars, and traffic laws exist.

Everything is dependent and integrated because there is no way to be independent or autonomous. Everything depends on everything else. We have simply taken the accountability out of the equation.

In days past, if we were in a tight-knit community and knew we were dependent on each other, it was very obvious if someone did something that was going to impact the community. Everyone would feel it, and that put a certain amount of responsibility on every individual as part of the whole. But now that is gone. We each have the safety nets of an indifferent government, insurance programs, and even more programs that insure we do not have to be accountable to each other and our community for our actions. We just have to make sure we have the premium paid, or that we have enough money in the bank.

It is this lack of accountability that leads to allowance of policies that favor wealth accumulation over the needs of others, and indifference of our neighbor's suffering, making it easier to compete with them for resources and jobs.

So what is the answer to the man's question: What must I do to inherit eternal life? Jesus teaches us that salvation is about becoming. Becoming a person and community that is shaped by covenant. A community that knows how to care and share with one another because in that other person we can see the image of God. A community that is willing to follow Jesus in the difficult job of breaking free from our world's way of self-interest and adopting our Lord's way of self-sacrificial love for one another. Only then will we fit into the Kingdom of God. Jesus did not charge his followers to get others to say the sinner's prayer. Jesus charged his followers to make disciples of people from all nations by teaching them to obey all that Jesus taught and to bring them into the community of faith by baptizing them. This is how we participate in eternal life, both now and in the future redemption of all creation at the resurrection of the faithful.

> It is easier for a camel to go through the eye of a needle than for someone who is rich to enter the kingdom of God. (Mark 10:25)

This shocking pronouncement has caused more than one pastor to try to soften its blow. The most common interpretation I have heard to alter its seriousness is to claim that there was a narrow gate into Jerusalem that would be difficult to get a camel through, and this gate was named needle. There is no evidence of this gate existing. Attempts to soften this challenging statement of Jesus distort the very meaning we have just covered, and make it so the wealthy that this verse is directed toward do not face the requirements of life shaped by covenant.

Additionally, because Jesus said "someone who is rich" we cannot take this passage as referring only to the man who asked the question. The challenge to live by the covenant and rethink wealth apply to all who would seek to follow Jesus. You may think that it would take an act of God to transform people to the extent that Jesus is calling for, and you would be right. This is the same thing that the disciples were thinking.

"Then Who Can Be Saved?"

> They were greatly astounded and said to one another, "Then who can be saved?" Jesus looked at them and said, "For mortals it is impossible, but not for God; for God all things are possible." (Mark 10:26-27)

Left to ourselves, we are incapable of restoring a right relationship between people and creation. God brings a perspective from beyond ourselves that allows us to see the injustice of our self-interested practices—in much the same way that Jesus, in love, helped the man to see the problem of wealth. God introduces creative options for moving towards shalom. Possibilities where nothing seemed possible. The possibility of God enables humans (mortals), to do the impossible. For us to do the impossible requires that we allow ourselves to hear God's gentle, loving call to the way of shalom.

Hearing the revelation of God is one thing, taking action is another. The man was not willing to act on what Jesus said. Just because we hear what God presents as the creative way forward does not mean we can envision it. Like the man who is challenged to leave his wealth, we are quick to question: how will this work? What if others take advantage of me? What if the other disciples do not follow through on their part? What will happen to my family? It is not hard to understand why the man lowered his head and walked away from Jesus.

Part of the issue for the man was that he came in challenging Jesus from the beginning, possibly to justify his participation with the elite. Because of this, the man heard the call to leave his wealth, but he did not hear the love from which the call came. He did not grasp that he was not called to do this alone, and that Jesus was inviting him to be restored to the community.

"Receive a Hundredfold Now in This Age"

> Peter began to say to him, "Look, we have left everything and followed you." Jesus said, "Truly I tell you, there is no one who has left house or brothers or sisters or mother or father or children or fields, for my sake and for the sake of the good news, who will not

receive a hundredfold now in this age—houses, brothers and sisters, mothers and children, and fields, with persecutions—and in the age to come eternal life." (Mark 10:28-30)

Jesus introduced a new phrase in this passage: "the good news." The good news is also translated as gospel. Often the gospel or good news is conflated with Jesus, as in the gospel or good news about Jesus. This makes Jesus the subject of the good news; however, in this passage Jesus talks about the sake of his name, and the sake of the good news. If Jesus is not talking about the good news of himself, what good news, or gospel, is Jesus talking about? For Jesus, the subject of the gospel or good news, is the Kingdom of God—the way of shalom. For example, at the beginning of Jesus' ministry, after the arrest of John the Baptist, we read:

> Now after John was arrested, Jesus came to Galilee, proclaiming the good news of God, and saying, "The time is fulfilled, and the kingdom of God has come near; repent, and believe in the good news." (Mark 1:14-15)

When we hear of the gospel of Jesus, this is referring to the good news that Jesus proclaimed and enacted in his life. The good news that a time is coming in which all will experience a life of abundance and fullness. The good news that Jesus lived a life of resistance to the Domination System and healing to the oppressed. The good news that we can participate in the way of shalom now, that we can follow Jesus in the way of the Sacred Revolution!

Now let's look at the rest of this passage. Peter is making a statement, which is really a question, that all followers of Jesus ask, "what is going to happen to us if we follow you in this crazy mission against the Domination System?" Jesus begins by acknowledging that following him can be costly. It may cost us the most important people and things in our life:

our house or fields, our brothers or sisters, our mother or father, or even our children. Not exactly an easy sell! Could you imagine a friend coming to invite you to their church with these words:

"Listen, there's this group I'm meeting with, but it could be bad for me if anyone finds out. You and I are friends so I can trust you, and I think you will get the importance of what we are up to. We are organizing a new kind of community that has the ability to heal our broken lives. The healing comes by breaking free of the dog-eat-dog way of our world, breaking free from the need to have more, breaking free from indifference to those who are suffering. But not everyone likes what we are doing. They are upset at our changing the way things have always been, for challenging the system that they are invested in and are successful at. Some of us have had their families turn their backs on them. Other have lost their jobs. I know that you know how important it is for the system to change. Too many are suffering so that a few can live like kings. Would you consider coming to one of our meetings?"

I would have loved to get an invitation like that! Instead all I hear is, "come check out how good our band is, the pastor is really funny, we have a great program for kids." No wonder people are bored with church. There is no point. On the other hand, what Jesus invites us to is risky and actually matters! When we start to question the way things are because Jesus has challenged us to confront injustice and oppression, people get uncomfortable, scared, and angry. People do not like change, especially if they are invested or benefit from the way things are.

As long as we live in a world where oppression and brutality are built into the systems we live within, following Jesus will entail the risk of losing jobs and family. God is not pointlessly nitpicking laws to see if we will obey. The things that God is concerned about are the things that lead to oppression and injustice of people made in God's image.

This is also why we cannot view persecution as a sign that we are doing something wrong. I have heard people counsel others that if something is going to cost you your family or job, it must not be God's will because God would not want you to lose those things. If that were true, we would have to throw out the Bible. Jesus was certainly doing the will of God and it cost him everything. And Jesus called us to follow him, to pick up our cross and follow. It is not that God wants anyone to suffer, but if we are unwilling to stand up for what is right, even at the risk of personal suffering, then oppression and injustice will continue to rule the day.

Jesus tells his followers that anyone who has had to leave it all to follow him will receive a hundredfold now. The hundredfold return is referring to the community of followers that welcome all those who have had to leave family for the sake of Jesus. The followers are a new family, and together they become a home for those who no longer have one. The reality is that we cannot faithfully follow Jesus on our own. We need others that come alongside us for support and encouragement. In these communities of faithful followers, we model a taste of shalom. Sacred Communities that help others in their journey to follow Jesus, and provide an example to the world of the alternative that is possible.

Like the church we read about in Acts chapter 4, the Sacred Revolution seeks to live out the challenge that God gave in Deuteronomy: "There will, however, be no one in need among you" (Deuteronomy 15:4a). The priority is people over possession.

> Now the whole group of those who believed were of one heart and soul, and no one claimed private ownership of any possessions, but everything they owned was held in common. With great power the apostles gave their testimony to the resurrection of the Lord Jesus, and great grace was upon them all. There

was not a needy person among them, for as many as owned lands or houses sold them and brought the proceeds of what was sold. (Acts 4:32-34)

So this idea of a new family, of receiving that which we lost, of healing and becoming whole, is not about the afterlife. It is about the experience of life in communities in the present. And then when eternal life is mentioned, it is essentially the same thing, only ongoing.

Some are want to dismiss this as socialism, but that is not what we are talking about here. If I were to try and come up with a word for this type of arrangement, I would call it familyism. If I truly view you as my brother or sister, there is a responsibility that comes with that. It is not about trying to regulate some kind of forced equal distribution like you would have in socialism. Everybody's not equal in families, rather, in a healthy family, no one goes without the things they need. You do what you have to do to care for the family. And this is not viewed as taking away from my own well-being because my wellbeing is dependent on my family's well-being.

People will be offended by this new definition of family. They will not understand how your connections with others in the Sacred Revolution can be more important than biological family (that is when biological family is opposed to the way of Jesus); they will not understand how you are not playing the same financial game of acquisition and why you are not participating in the stock market; they will not understand why you are resisting the system. But they will not stop at not understanding. They will try to get you to conform to the way things are, to respect biological family and nation state policies. This is why Jesus said you will receive a new family and community, but with persecutions.

If you are still caught up in chasing wealth as a means of security, if you are not concerned with the implications of your lifestyle and the suffering it causes others, if you are unwilling to put people first over property, then you are not going to fit into God's vision of shalom.

It is not that anybody will be trying to keep you out—you are not going to want in. You are not going to want to be a part of that new world and new family because you are too focused on self and making sure you have got what you need. You will not be able to see or recognize the fact that we are all interdependent and that your wellbeing is dependent on my wellbeing.

This all may sound like turning the world upside down, and that is exactly what Jesus said. The first will be last and the last will be first. Welcome to the Sacred Revolution!

"First Will Be Last, and the Last Will Be First"

> But many who are first will be last, and the last will be first. (Mark 10:31)

The great reversal Jesus is talking about is not just swapping positions. It is not about the people on the bottom taking their place at the top of the current Domination System; rather, it is about the way of shalom ascending over the way of empire.

The hope of those who love God is that we will be resurrected at the end of this age, and we will participate in the redeemed creation in which all the walls of separation have been torn down. God will dwell with God's people. Love and mercy will rule the day and we will once again partake of the tree of life. This is the Kingdom of God, shalom actualized. This is the future made possible through Jesus' nonviolent confrontation with the Domination System. Not only is the hope of shalom in the future made sure by the resurrection, but we are liberated in the present in order to create outposts of shalom now, as a witness to a world that cannot conceive of God's way. We are enlisted to continue in Jesus' nonviolent confrontation of domination systems. We are given hope for the future and a community in the present, in which we can experience genuine connection and healing, and real-life adventure as we creatively find ways to confront the powers that be.

A Time of Peace

The prophets give us glimpses of what shalom will look like. They entice us and leave us wanting more, but they are painting a picture of our future. In the book of Revelation we hear that those who persist in the institutions of the kingdom of the world will finally have to answer for their oppression of the weak and their policies that cause starvation and the destruction of the earth:

> There were loud voices in heaven, saying, "The kingdom of the world has become the kingdom of our Lord and of his Messiah, and he will reign forever and ever." Then the twenty-four elders who sit on their thrones before God fell on their faces and worshipped God, singing, "We give you thanks, Lord God Almighty, who are and who were, for you have taken your great power and begun to reign. The nations raged, but your wrath has come, and the time for judging the dead, for rewarding your servants, the prophets and saints and all who fear your name, both small and great, and for destroying those who destroy the earth." (Revelation 11:15-18)

The answer to the brutality of the world is twofold: the first is our witness of an alternative way of life in the present—confronting systems of domination. The second is in the end those who persist in their inhuman ways will have to answer for their actions. The way of life being established by God is in stark contrast to the current order of the world:

Then I saw a new heaven and a new earth... And I heard a loud voice from the throne saying, "See, the home of God is among [people]. He will dwell with them; they will be his peoples, and God himself will be with them; he will wipe every tear from their eyes. Death will be no more; mourning and crying and pain will be no more, for the first things have passed away." And the one who was seated on the throne said, "See, I am making all things new." Also he said, "Write this, for these words are trustworthy and true." (Revelation 21:1-5)

Then the angel showed me the river of the water of life, bright as crystal, flowing from the throne of God and of the Lamb through the middle of the street of the city. On either side of the river is the tree of life with its twelve kinds of fruit, producing its fruit each month; and the leaves of the tree are for the healing of the nations. (Revelation 22:1-2)

God will once again dwell with us as it was in the garden, and the tree of life will be open to us so that we can partake in life to the fullest. Its leaves are for the healing of the nations. Isaiah offers additional visions of this future:

In days to come the mountain of the Lord's house shall be established as the highest of the mountains, and shall be raised above the hills; all the nations shall stream to it. Many peoples shall come and say, "Come, let us go up to the mountain of the Lord, to the house of the God of Jacob; that he may teach us his ways and that we may walk in his paths." For out of Zion shall go forth instruction, and the word of the Lord from Jerusalem. He shall judge between the nations, and shall arbitrate for many peoples; they shall beat their swords into ploughshares, and their spears into pruning-hooks;

nation shall not lift up sword against nation, neither shall they learn war any more. (Isaiah 2:2-4)

The wolf shall live with the lamb, the leopard shall lie down with the kid, the calf and the lion and the fatling together, and a little child shall lead them. The cow and the bear shall graze, their young shall lie down together; and the lion shall eat straw like the ox. The nursing child shall play over the hole of the asp, and the weaned child shall put its hand on the adder's den. They will not hurt or destroy on all my holy mountain; for the earth will be full of the knowledge of the Lord as the waters cover the sea. (Isaiah 11:6-9)

On this mountain the Lord of hosts will make for all peoples a feast of rich food, a feast of well-aged wines, of rich food filled with marrow, of well-aged wines strained clear. And he will destroy on this mountain the shroud that is cast over all peoples, the sheet that is spread over all nations; he will swallow up death forever. Then the Lord God will wipe away the tears from all faces, and the disgrace of his people he will take away from all the earth, for the Lord has spoken. It will be said on that day, Lo, this is our God; we have waited for him, so that he might save us. This is the Lord for whom we have waited; let us be glad and rejoice in his salvation. For the hand of the Lord will rest on this mountain. (Isaiah 25:6-10)

The instruction of the Lord brings peace and the end of war. Can you imagine the nations taking their instruments of destruction and turning them into tools to grow food! We may wonder at the vision of lions eating straw, but the point is that not only will humans end their practice of violence but nature itself will no longer be hostile. There is wholeness in the age of shalom. The world will be brought to the way it was always intended to be. Mary, the mother of Jesus, recognized the significance of Jesus coming into the world as the Messiah of God. She knew this was the beginning of the great reversal. She sang:

> My soul magnifies the Lord, and my spirit rejoices in God my Savior... His mercy is for those who fear him from generation to generation. He has shown strength with his arm; he has scattered the proud in the thoughts of their hearts. He has brought down the powerful from their thrones, and lifted up the lowly; he has filled the hungry with good things, and sent the rich away empty. (Luke 1:46-53)

The first will be last, and the last first. The coming of the Kingdom of God means that we will be restored to life in the way it should be. There will be no more rich abusing the poor, no more hunger because people refuse to share, no more senseless destruction of the earth for profit. Creation itself will be redeemed as Paul shares with us:

> I consider that the sufferings of this present time are not worth comparing with the glory about to be revealed to us. For the creation waits with eager longing for the revealing of the children of God; for the creation was subjected to futility, not of its own will but by the will of the one who subjected it, in hope that the creation itself will be set free from its bondage to decay and will obtain the freedom of the glory of the children of God. We know that the whole creation has been groaning in labor pains until now; and not only the creation, but we ourselves, who have the first fruits of the Spirit, groan inwardly while we wait for adoption, the redemption of our bodies. (Romans 8:18-23)

God promises to provide what we need, freeing us from the temptation to hold back from giving to others. As Jesus said:

> Therefore do not worry, saying, "What will we eat?" or "What will we drink?" or "What will we wear?" For it is the Gentiles who strive for all these things; and indeed your heavenly Father knows that you need all these things. But strive first for the kingdom of God and his righteousness, and all these things will be given to you as well. (Matthew 6:31-33)

It is in seeking first the Kingdom of God that we become a community that knows how to share and care for one another as brothers and sisters. This is how our needs are met. God is not some genie in the sky granting our wishes. God calls people to be truly human, and when people hear and answer that call, we learn how to treat one another with care and respect. Jesus taught us to pray saying:

> Your kingdom come, your will be done, on earth as it is in heaven. (Matthew 6:10)

As disciples of Jesus, we look forward to the restoration of the earth when God's Kingdom is established and justice and mercy rule the day. When people are devoted to their creator and learn to love God with all their might and their neighbor as themselves. However, it is not enough to long for that day, we are commissioned to do God's will right here and now, on earth as it is in heaven. To that end, we are to become a community of disciples who are learning together how to live. We are not just offering an idea to a confused and hurting world; rather, we are becoming a tangible example of what it looks like when people live together in faithfulness to their God. We are in fact ambassadors of the Kingdom. This is what church is supposed to be!

Fear is the natural response when considering the extensive change we are called to as disciples in the Sacred Revolution. We are called to leave the security of the world and our culture in order to embrace the foreign risky faith of following Jesus into the way of shalom. Without departure from the way things are, there is no hope for the revival of true humanity and the end of brutality. This radical change in how we live is what is meant by the word: repentance.

> Jesus came to Galilee, proclaiming the good news of God, and saying, "The time is fulfilled, and the kingdom of God has come near; repent, and believe in the good news." (Mark 1:14-15)

What is the motivation that leads us to true repentance and transformation of our life? Gratitude. Gratitude for what God has done in the creation and redemption of the world. Gratitude for what God is making possible in the present: transformation of our lives from the hopelessness of brutality and loneliness, to lives of meaning made whole in community. And gratitude for the future hope of shalom made sure by God through the work of Jesus.

God's beauty shines through the brutality and luxury of this world. It has the power to so transform us that we can be determined to follow Jesus into the shalom way of life no matter what the cost. And in our faithfulness we will discover that God is gentle with us. This does not mean that the way of faithfulness is not hard—it is! But God does not expect us to have it all together overnight. God is patient with us. God does not leave us to our own devices. We are empowered by the Spirit and shaped by worship into the people God desires us to be, relearning what it means to be human. On this journey we discover that our desire for community is becoming reality. A community where we are accepted, respected, and valued. We understand that none of us can do this by ourselves—we need each other.

As we are in the process of being formed into God's people, we discover ways to work for God's vision of justice. This may involve simple things like changing who we support by how we spend our money. If companies are involved in practices that we would never personally condone, we need to be aware that it is our money making those policies possible. Our change may involve exploring foundational changes in how we live more sustainably as a community. Our faith journey is one of worship, prayer, study, and fellowship, but it is also an adventure that engages us in every aspect of life. At times, the way of shalom is very hard, but it is always rewarding. What we are doing has meaning and significance beyond the popular alternative of merely having a private relationship with God. We have been called to participate with God in the process of redeeming the world!

To transition from being people formed and shaped by our culture (focused on individualism and self-preservation) and into a people formed and shaped by God's vision of shalom is a process. If we are going to worship God in the way that God desires, and if we are going to practice authentic community, there is a lot for us to learn before we begin. Someone does not decide one day that they are a Christian and that is it. Jesus said that we are to make disciples by teaching them to obey everything he has taught us.

Part Three

Life in Community

"Now the whole group of those who believed were of one heart and soul, and no one claimed private ownership of any possessions, but everything they owned was held in common. With great power the apostles gave their testimony to the resurrection of the Lord Jesus, and great grace was upon them all. There was not a needy person among them, for as many as owned lands or houses sold them and brought the proceeds of what was sold. They laid it at the apostles' feet, and it was distributed to each as any had need."

   - Acts of the Apostles

THE PRIORITY OF GRATITUDE

The hardest part of losing our house was how long the process took. This was especially hard for my wife. Growing up she had to move from place to place, never living in a house owned by her parents. Some years after Michelle and I were married, when our children were four and seven, we bought our first house together. It was the first house my wife had ever lived in that was not rented. And now we were losing it.

A year after we bought the house I was laid off from my job. It was nearly a year before I got back on my feet. During that year we struggled to keep the house, but it was a losing battle. There was just no way to pay for it. We used all of our savings and maxed out our debt before we were forced to sell. I did everything I could because the house had such a sentimental importance to my wife. We ate rice, beans, and potatoes almost every night. Like many couples that go through a crippling financial crisis, our marriage was put to the test. It was one of the hardest times in my life. My stress manifested in health problems that included a severe case of shingles; that is not a disease a young person is supposed to get.

It was during this failed attempt to keep the house that some dear friends of ours, Rob and Michelle, offered to watch the kids so my wife and I could go out and spend some much needed time together. I don't remember what we did—we didn't even have enough money to eat out. But I do remember how blessed we felt to have friends who cared about us. Their small act of kindness was a huge blessing.

When we got home our friends left quickly and I was worried we had stayed out too late. I figured I would call them the next day and make it right. My wife and I went into the kitchen for something to drink and when I looked in a cupboard I noticed food that wasn't there before. We checked in all the cupboards and the fridge and found food everywhere. We couldn't believe it. We experienced a truly magical moment and all we could do was hold each other and cry. Now I knew why they left so quickly! At that moment, we experienced profound gratitude. I looked for ways we could thank them, but nothing seemed adequate. It was many years ago, but the thought of their kindness still brings tears to my eyes. I thank God for the gift Rob and Michelle brought into our lives!

Definition of Gratitude

Rob and Michelle did not fill our cupboards of food expecting us to do the same in return—we couldn't have. But even though we could not do for them what they did for us, we were still able to show them how much we appreciated them and valued them as our friends. This exchange illustrates an important aspect of gratitude. Within a relationship there is a possibility of reciprocity, where there is giving and receiving. As a recipient of a gift, I may not be able to repay with a gift of the same value, but I will feel an intense loyalty to the relationship and have a desire to express my gratitude for the gift in tangible ways that the giver will appreciate. If I fail to demonstrate loyalty and gratitude to the giver, I am displaying ingratitude, which is an insult to the relationship. I am sure that Rob and Michelle did not have any expectations of us, they just wanted to freely give a gift to their friends. But what would have happened to our friendship if I responded to their gift with ingratitude? What if I did not acknowledge what they did in any way? How would you feel if you were Rob or Michelle and I responded that way? Giving gifts can be done freely and without expectations, save for one: that gratitude be demonstrated to the giver, showing that they and their gift are appreciated.

How Does Gratitude Relate to the Sacred Revolution?

The Sacred Revolution increases our awareness of the injustice and oppression inherent in the Domination System in which we live. If we are not careful, that knowledge can cause us to become bitter and tempt us toward retaliation and away from reconciliation and the vision of shalom. That is why developing an attitude of gratitude is one of the top three priorities of the Sacred Revolution.

The example above of Rob and Michelle left out an important piece of context—it took place within a faith community. God changes the equation in the gift/gratitude cycle, but we need to understand how gratitude worked in Jesus' day before we can appreciate the radical shift in how Jesus and his followers practiced gratitude.

Gratitude

We will start with a basic definition of gratitude as it would have been known in Jesus' day. Gratitude is the experience of obligation in response to a gift received. The obligation is to show your appreciation in tangible ways to the giver, and that are appropriate to the gift. The response is not always expected to be equal to the gift, but still of value to the giver.

In the Greek language used to write the New Testament, there is one word for both gift and for giving thanks for the gift: charis. When referring to the giving of a gift or favor, charis is often translated as grace. In English, we see charis show up in the words charisma (someone who is gifted), and charismatic (exercising the gifts of the spirit). When referring to the response of receiving a gift, charis is often translated as thanks. In English, we see charis in the word Eucharist. The Eucharist is literally a thanksgiving meal. Our English word gratitude comes from Latin in which there is also one word for both gift and gratitude: gratia.

Both charis and gratia refer to the cycle of gift and gratitude—a reciprocal flow from the giver to the receiver and back to the giver. Charis is a tangible object or service, and gratitude for a gift is expected to be tangible as well. This is not necessarily a cycle of equality. When the gift is greater than the recipient can repay, this requires that the recipient remembers the gift. The inequality of the gift and response creates an ongoing relationship between the two parties. If the gift can be repaid in equal value, then the exchange is complete and there is no further need for gifts. This kind of cycle is used amongst equals. Within the gift/gratitude cycle, to forget your obligation is to be ungrateful or an ingrate, and not remembering is a serious affront to the relationship.

You Didn't Build It

An unusual event happened back in 2012. You might recall a phrase that was getting bantered back and forth in the political arena that said, "If you've got a business—you didn't build that. Somebody else made that happen." Like most things that happen in political debates, this got taken completely out of context.

The reason this phrase gave Conservative candidates so much fuel was because it seemed as though it was challenging some fundamental ideas we hold in the United States: the idea that one is able to make their own way in this world, is able to be a self-made person, and is able to create a path to what and where one wants to go in this world.

What did Obama mean when he said, "If you've got a business—you didn't build that. Somebody else made that happen"? In the face of our extremely individualized way of thinking about ourselves, Obama was challenging us to reflect on how interconnected and dependent we all are, even in the United States. Whatever we think we have done, we have to remember that the only reason we are able to do it is because of all the efforts of other people that have come before us.

If you are a business owner, how are people able to reach your business? They are driving on roads that the government made and paid for. Your ability to exchange money for goods is due to the economic system. The ability for you to communicate with your customers is a result of education. Customers have money to buy your goods because they are working at other businesses. There is a reasonably stable society because of police, fire, and emergency services that allow consumers to feel safe enough to spend money and enjoy your goods.

That is not to say that what one contributes as an individual is insignificant. There are certainly wonderful inventions and services that individuals have come up with that benefit many of us, but we have to recognize that everything we do is only possible because of all the systems, knowledge, and inventions that already exist. Obama was helping us to have a greater appreciation for what the government makes possible and how truly interconnected we all are. "If you've got a business—you didn't build that. Somebody else made that happen."

Is there any way to be truly independent? What if I ran away to live in the woods and built my own log cabin, completely off the grid? But if I chop down trees to make that cabin using an ax, I had to have gotten that tool from somewhere. Sure, I could go find a rock and chisel an ax head, but even then I received the knowledge of how to do that from an outside source. There is nothing that we have done where we have been completely on our own. We are all connected and dependent in countless ways, beginning at birth.

Our culture is focused on individualism, innovation, and the future, and as a result we wrestle with historical amnesia. We tend to forget how much we have received from others. We have lost a sense of gratitude.

Additionally, our economy is based on consumerism. It must generate a void in order to produce an incessant need to consume or the system dies. As a result, we are daily bombarded with messages designed to create dissatisfaction as opposed to gratitude. The system requires us to be dissatisfied so that we will try consuming another self-help program, or the next new product, or move to a new location, or take a vacation, or whatever it is we are being sold that promises to fill the void that has been created by the media and marketing systems.

The antidote to an oversaturation of individualistic cravings is gratitude, and we develop gratitude by remembering.

Patron/Client Relationships and Charis in the Roman Empire

Let's look at how patron/client relationships played out in the world of Jesus. For nearly one hundred years Israel had existed under Roman occupation, and for over three hundred years it was surrounded by Greek culture. This had a profound effect on how people lived, and transformed the Israelite culture in countless ways; specifically, the grace/gratitude cycle as expressed in the Roman patronage system came to predominate among the Israelite elite. Patronage represents the giver of the gift (charis/grace) as a patron (meaning father), and the receiver as a client who is indebted to show gratitude to the patron. This cycle is known as the patron/client system.

The patron/client relationship was at the core of the Roman economy. Knowing to whom you owed gratitude was a primary ethical concern. To fail to remember was a serious moral failure, if not an actual crime. Memory is essential to maintaining gratitude.

Gratitude to Parents
At the top of the list of things you should remember in the ancient world are your parents. They have given you the

ultimate gift of life. It is believed, then, that everything that comes after birth is owed in part to your parents.

Gratitude to Family

In addition to remembering the gift of life from your parents, one was expected to remember their family and all that family provides. In the ancient Mediterranean world, family kinship is essential to everything. You do not forget family and you do not turn your back on family.

Gratitude to Government

The concept of family was extended to political structures. The family became a metaphor for the government. Caesar fancied himself as the father of Rome. Rome was considered a "household." Our word for "economy" comes from the Greek word for household, oikonomos (oiko – house; nomos – rule or law).

When Rome was at its most influential was called Pax Romana, meaning The Peace of Rome. This period of time saw rich trade and commerce, and people existed in relative safety. This was a tremendous blessing that came with an expectation of a debt of gratitude. Fulfilling these expectations was a part of being a Roman citizen.

Gratitude to Patrons

The role of a patron (father), was to allow relationships that could cross social classes. Normally there would be no relationships outside of a particular honor status or class. In the ancient world there was no middle class; there were the elite, a limited number of artisans who helped support the elite class, and then everyone else. The elite class was somewhere between 2-5% of the population, while the majority were what we would consider lower class. But there were many beggars and day laborers, among others, who had it even worse. This group was around 10-15% of the population and was considered "disposable."

Patrons could grant gifts (charis) to those in lower classes. They were called clients. The client would then have an obligation to the patron for these gifts. At the very least this obligation would include a responsibility to honor the patron. The patron/client relationship formed the bedrock of the Roman economy. Beginning at the top with Caesar, and all the way down from him, gifts were given to create obligations or indebtedness. This required remembering to whom gratitude was owed. The relationship between the patron and clients was often referred to as a "friendship," where a client became "friends" with the patron (father).

It is interesting to note how these words that we associate with religious concepts are from the economic sphere of life. The "Father" that gives "grace" to whom we are expected to give "thanks." It is only in modern times that we have conceived of an economic sphere as separate from the religious sphere.

In the Roman world, to forget a debt was considered a culpable sin that could be punished. If one failed to remember, it was assumed that some vice was at work in the person, such as greed or a wicked desire for advancement. Everything was based upon this idea of becoming "indebted" to others, and to mess with this debt system (gratitude), was to threaten the very fabric of Roman society.

The patron/client and honor systems have persisted remarkably well from Mediterranean times to modern day. An excellent way to get a sense of how all this worked is to watch the movie *The Godfather*. Look at the opening scene and notice the use of honor, debt, father, favor, gift, and friendship.

In the opening scene of *The Godfather*, the character Bonasera asks Vito Corleone to murder two men in the name of justice, avenging his daughter. Rather than granting his request, Corleone states that Bonasera is no friend of his, so why should he grant requests: "...You come to me and you say, 'Don Corleone, give me justice.' But you don't ask with respect. You don't offer friendship. You don't even think to call me Godfather. Instead, you come into my house on the day my daughter is to be married, and you ask me to do murder for money." By offering Corleone money rather than friendship in exchange for having the two men murdered, Bonarera shows disrespect. In the end, it is a kiss on the hand and a promise of a future deed in exchange for Corleone's "favor" that grants Bonarera the lives of the men he wishes dead: "Some day, and that day may never come, I'll call upon you to do a service for me. But uh, until that day—accept this justice as a gift on my daughter's wedding day."

In our time, when we hear about people in government positions receiving gifts from powerful people or corporations, we are concerned that the politician will feel indebted and this will impact their decision making. We see this as horrible and corrupt, and as something that needs to be rooted out. In the ancient Roman world this was business as usual. It was not considered corruption because there was no other way to conduct business. That was the way it worked. Jesus and his followers brought something very different to the Roman world.

Perceived in Gratitude

> And call no one your father on earth, for you have one Father, the one in heaven. (Matthew 23:9)

Sometimes Christian groups have taken this to mean you are not supposed to call a priest "father," but this verse has nothing to do with that. In fact, there are other places where Paul considered himself a father to churches that he had started (1 Corinthians 4:15).

When Jesus is saying "call no one your father," he is dealing with this issue of patronage, in the patron-client relationship. He is telling his followers not to participate in the patron/client cycle because there is only one father (literally God-Father), and that is where the real gifts of grace come from. You only owe a debt of gratitude to God. The implications of this were staggering for those living in the Roman world.

In the Sermon on the Mount Jesus says, "Give to everyone who begs from you, and do not refuse anyone who wants to borrow from you" (Matthew 5:42). This is not a call for Jesus' followers to become doormats or let people take everything from them; he is saying do not give while expecting to receive something in return. Or, more accurately, do not give with the purpose of causing someone to become indebted to you.

The behavior of Jesus and his followers threatened the very fabric of the empire. Tacitus wrote about an instigation of the Christians in Rome leading to Emperor Claudius kicking the Jews out of Rome. Tacitus referred to the Jesus followers as "haters of humanity" because they threatened the idea of friendship—the patron/client bond that held everybody together.

In Acts the followers are "turning the world upside down" (Acts 17:6). When the followers start breaking with patronage, you can bet it would be seen as turning their world upside down.

Jesus also challenged the obligations that people would be expected to have toward family: "Another of the disciples said to him, 'Lord, first let me go and bury my father.' But Jesus said to him, 'Follow me, and let the dead bury their own dead'" (Matthew 9:21-22). One's obligation to care for a father, especially at the time of death, would be considered a primary responsibility for the child—a final act of respect in gratitude for the gift of life. To say that someone should leave that obligation would have seemed heretical.

Jesus says in Matthew 10:34-39: "Do not think that I have come to bring peace to the earth. I have not come to bring peace but a sword, for I have come to set a man against his father, and a daughter against her mother, and a daughter-in-law against her mother-in-law. And one's foes will be members of one's own household. Whoever loves Father or Mother more than me is not worthy of me. And whoever loves son or daughter more than me is not worthy of me. And whoever does not take up the cross and follow me is not worthy of me. Those who find their life will lose it, and those who lose their life for my sake will find it."

In Luke 14:26, Jesus says, "Whoever comes to me and does not hate father and mother, wife and children, brothers and sisters, yes, and even life itself, cannot be my disciple." These are strong words in a culture that is bound by the obligation to family. For Jesus to suggest that to be faithful to him you have to be willing to break the bonds of commitment to your biological family and replace it with a new family defined in Jesus must have sounded insane to his followers. This was a complete undermining of their whole way of life. These passages have sometimes gone right over our heads because we have not seen the significance of what these statements mean coming from the context of Jesus' world.

Jesus Regarding the Cycle of Grace and Gratitude

The source of grace that we need to remember and show gratitude for is above the Emperor, family, and patrons (fathers) of any kind. The ultimate source of grace is God. "Father" as it is applied to God is not about gender, it is about fulfilling the role of the true and ultimate patron. It is our reflection on, and remembrance of, all the many gifts of God that form the basis for our gratitude. Any gift that a human can give is only possible because of the foundational gifts of God; therefore, we are indebted to God alone and any secondary benefits we receive from others cannot create a debt that overrides our primary debt to God.

Jesus teaches that when you give a luncheon or a dinner, you should not invite your friends, brothers, relatives, or rich neighbors, in case they may invite you in return, and you would be repaid. But when you give a banquet, invite the poor, the crippled, the lame, and the blind. You will be blessed, because they cannot repay you, for you will be repaid at the resurrection of the righteous (Luke 14:12-14).

> Beware of practicing your piety before others in order to be seen by them; for then you have no reward from your Father in heaven. So whenever you give alms, do not sound a trumpet before you, as the hypocrites do in the synagogues and in the streets, so that they may be praised by others. Truly I tell you, they have received their reward. But when you give alms, do not let your left hand know what your right hand is doing, so that your alms may be done in secret; and your Father who sees in secret will reward you. (Matthew 6:1-4)

Jesus will go on in this passage to say that when you are doing your prayers, do not do it out in the public to gain recognition from everybody else, but rather speak them in privacy. He says, "Your Father who sees in secret will reward you."

He asks that we not cause others to become indebted to us by the goodwill we do. We are to do good for others because of the gifts that God has given us. Jesus says that God will complete the grace/gratitude cycle when we give to others that cannot repay us. This is a return to how the grace cycle functions according to the Torah in which God owns everything. We own nothing and are simply here for a short time, functioning as stewards. As God's representatives—his image on Earth—we have the responsibility to reflect to the world who our Father is. And how does God treat the world? Again, from Jesus:

> You have heard that it was said, "You shall love your neighbor and hate your enemy." But I say to you, Love your enemies and pray for those who persecute you, so that you may be children of your Father in heaven; for he makes his sun rise on the evil and on the good, and

sends rain on the righteous and on the unrighteous. For if you love those who love you, what reward do you have? Do not even the tax collectors do the same? And if you greet only your brothers and sisters, what more are you doing than others? Do not even the Gentiles do the same? Be perfect, therefore, as your heavenly Father is perfect. (Matthew 5:43-48)

The way that God expects us to express gratitude for God's gifts is in how we treat each other. Our obligation to practice brotherly/sisterly love—to recognize each other as brother and sister—is how we demonstrate gratitude to God for the gifts we have received.

Paul, picking up the agenda from Jesus, says, "Owe no one anything..." Again, think about how this would sound in a society in which everyone is indebted to others from birth and are expected to remember it. "Owe no one anything, except to love one another, for the one who loves another has fulfilled the law" (Romans 13:8).

Paul also wrote, "And let the peace of Christ rule in your hearts which indeed you were called in one body and be thankful" (Colossians 3:15). "Rejoice always, pray without ceasing. Give thanks in all circumstances, for this is the will of God in Christ Jesus for you" (1 Thessalonians 5:16-18). According to Paul, giving thanks (gratitude) to God is a core part of our walk with Jesus.

It is interesting to notice that at the beginning of Romans, Paul seems to imply that the original sin, if you will, of Adam and Eve was ingratitude. He says, "For though they knew God, they did not honor Him as God or give thanks to Him. But they became futile in their thinking, and their senseless minds were darkened" (Romans 1:21).

Gratitude and the Sacred Revolution

Gratitude is essential to the Sacred Revolution for two key reasons. First, gratitude helps to keep us from bitterness and vengeance. Maintaining a sense of gratitude requires us to remember and reflect on the gift of life, the intricacies and interconnectedness of all things, and how small we are in the grand scheme of things; and yet we are important to God. Second, the recognition that our debt of gratitude is owed to the ultimate source of all grace alone. This frees us from obligations, debts, or allegiances that would cause us to act contrary to the vision of shalom.

What makes a revolution a revolution is a change in allegiance. Jesus' insistence that gratitude is owed to God alone undermined and challenged the political allegiance to Rome, the basis of the economic system of his day, and the authority of the religious leaders. Gratitude to God alone forms the foundation for true humanity and God's vision of shalom, and it got Jesus killed. But his death was not the end of the story.

The resurrection of Jesus was God's confirmation that Jesus was, in fact, the fullest revelation of God and the way of shalom. The resurrection of Jesus also demonstrated that the empire's power to kill is no match for God's power of life. And the resurrection assures us that our work for shalom is not in vain. We are promised that the way of shalom will ultimately prevail and the faithful who have worked and died in pursuit of shalom will experience resurrection and life in a world brought to its intended state. Certainly this is another cause for gratitude—to give thanks that we will inherit a world run by shalom, or what the Bible refers to as The Kingdom of God.

> Therefore, since we are receiving a kingdom that cannot be shaken, let us give thanks, by which we offer to God an acceptable worship with reverence and awe; for indeed our God is a consuming fire.
> (Hebrews 12:28-29)

According to the author of Hebrews, our response to the promise of God's Kingdom of shalom is to "give thanks," or show gratitude. And the form our gratitude should take, or how our gratitude should be demonstrated, is in acts of worship that are acceptable and pleasing to God. Our worship will also show our reverence for God. How do we express our gratitude in acts of worship that are acceptable to God?

We are not left on our own to try to figure out what God finds acceptable. The next passage of Hebrews gives us several examples, which I will cover in some detail in the next few sections of this book. But first let's review the context for our relationship with God. The nature of our relationship helps make sense out of what God finds acceptable.

Our relationship is defined by covenant. The type of covenant that forms the foundation of our relationship with God and other people is a kinship-style covenant. This means that we bond to each other as a family. As a family, we have obligations and expectations of each other, and these are defined in the covenant. This core covenant is found in Exodus 20:1-17, which we commonly refer to as the Ten Commandments, or in Hebrew, the Ten Words.

When we are living up to our covenantal obligations we are considered righteous; that is, we are in right standing with one another and God. When we fail to live up to our covenantal obligations there is a breakdown in the relationship. The brokenness of the relationship is called sin. When we work to make the relationship right again, this is called rightification, which is not a word in English so we translated it as justification. The sin has been justified, meaning that the relationship has been restored to right standing.

The concern for keeping and fulfilling the covenant obligations is captured in the Hebrew word "hesed." Often hesed is translated as "steadfast love" in the Old Testament. Throughout the Psalms, you will hear a refrain celebrating

God's steadfast love. These passages are praising God for his faithfulness to the covenant even when we fail. When God acts out of loyalty to the covenant, or when we act out of loyalty to the covenant, this is referred to as hesed.

> For I [God] desire steadfast love [hesed] and not sacrifice, the knowledge of God rather than burnt offerings. (Hosea 6:6)

Here God is saying through the prophet Hosea that God would rather we act in loyalty to the covenant (hesed) than try to fix failure through sacrifice. When this critical concept of hesed gets imported into the Greek language of the New Testament, the word hesed (steadfast love) is translated as mercy, as we can see in this verse from Matthew:

> Go and learn what this means, 'I desire mercy, not sacrifice.' (Matthew 9:13)

In this comment from Jesus directed at the Pharisees, we see Hosea's passage quoted and mercy is used to translate hesed. In another important teaching we see mercy as the expected response from someone who has received mercy:

> Should you not have had mercy on your fellow slave, as I had mercy on you? (Matthew 18:33)

In this parable a person—let's call him Joe—receives mercy from his master when an unpayable debt is forgiven. Joe then promptly throws one of his own servants into debtors prison for not repaying a much smaller debt to Joe. The master questions Joe, asking him why Joe did not show mercy to his servant in the same way that the master showed mercy to Joe. It was expected that because Joe received the gift of debt forgiveness that he would show gratitude for the gift by showing mercy to others who needed it from Joe.

When Joe did not show mercy, he was demonstrating ingratitude. This ingratitude ruptured the relationship between Joe and his master to the point that Joe missed out on his own gift of mercy and was thrown into debtors prison himself.

Gratitude is the experience of obligation in response to receiving a gift that cannot be repaid. It is demonstrated in tangible acts that are pleasing to the giver. What makes it so hard for us to be grateful and to recognize gifts we have received from God? We have received the gift of life and hope of shalom. From the beginning of your awareness in life, there has been an active campaign to shape your thinking and desires. The goal of this campaign is to have you dissatisfied with life regardless of your station or material possessions.

We live in a capitalistic, free market economic system. That system depends on unending consumption. If you become satisfied, you stop consuming and the system fails. The motivation of the system to keep you dissatisfied is so powerful that all means and costs are justified to keep you consuming. The insanity and blindness of the Domination System to continually feed the need for consumption is evident in the lack of concern in the destruction of the environment that is needed to sustain life. This insanity even finds ways to profit from the death and destruction of war. Often US corporations will sell arms to both sides of a conflict.

If the Domination System will not stop the insanity that could destroy all life on the planet in its quest for profit, it will not stop at using you for its own purposes. We are all affected by the consumer system so completely we do not always recognize that our desires are not our own. We have come to think that the consumer self is the real self. It is not until we take an active role resisting the Domination System's education methods and refuse to participate in the consumption game that we have a chance to break free from our false desires. These desires are manufactured for us by the religion of the Domination System.

In contrast to the religion of the Domination System, we are offered an unshakable kingdom—a world shaped by shalom. The phrase "unshakable" is making a reference to a passage from the prophet Haggai:

> For thus says the Lord of hosts: Once again, in a little while, I will shake the heavens and the earth and the sea and the dry land; and I will shake all the nations, so that the treasure of all nations shall come, and I will fill this house with splendor, says the Lord of hosts.
> (Haggai 2:6-7)

At the time of Haggai, the Israelites were working to rebuild their life in Israel after returning from their captivity in Babylon. Their attempt at rebuilding the temple seemed pathetic when compared to their memory of the first temple built by Solomon. God, through the prophet Haggai, addressed their feelings regarding the value of their work by showing them that the grandeur of the nations would not last, and what seemed to be their minor effort would stand in the end. In a similar way, our efforts in building our small and struggling faith communities can feel like that. But what we are building has more value to God than all the nations of the world that try to make life according to their vision rather than God's. All the nations will be shaken and all the precious resources they have hoarded, the resources that belong to God will come to the one thing in this world that will last—communities in which people are committed to Jesus' way of life. Since we are receiving a kingdom that cannot be shaken, let us show our gratitude.

The letter to the Hebrews goes on to say that gratitude needs to be shown in worship that is acceptable (or pleasing) to God and that shows reverence. In Chapter 13 of Hebrews the author shows us what that acceptable worship is. But before we explore what is said there, this passage closes with a caution: our God is a consuming fire! Here the author is quoting from Moses in Deuteronomy:

> So be careful not to forget the covenant that the Lord your God made with you, and not to make for yourselves an idol in the form of anything that the Lord your God has forbidden you. For the Lord your God is a devouring fire, a jealous God. (Deuteronomy 4:23-24)

It can become easy to think of God too casually. Do not be tempted. Our God is awesome, bestowing countless gifts, but God is not fooled by insincerity or manipulation. The magnitude of the gifts we have received from the source of all life, and the gift we are receiving in the Kingdom/Shalom of God, expects an appropriate response. That response is a total life commitment out of gratitude.

> For the love of Christ urges us on, because we are convinced that one has died for all; therefore all have died. And he died for all, so that those who live might live no longer for themselves, but for him who died and was raised for them. (2 Corinthians 5:14-15)

How Do You Offer Acceptable Worship?

We have explored Hebrews 12:28 and learned that our response to God's gift of the Kingdom is to "give thanks" or to "show gratitude," and that our demonstration of gratitude would form "acceptable/pleasing worship" to God. The question is now: how are we to offer acceptable worship? The author of Hebrews anticipated this question and proceeds in the next section of his book to give us some concrete examples of acceptable worship. We know these passages belong together because 12:28 begins with the phrase acceptable or pleasing to God, and concludes with a

111

phase about pleasing God in 13:16. The concept of pleasing God forms bookends around this section so that you will not miss the point. What is fascinating is that most of what is prescribed for us as pleasing to God has to do with how we treat each other!

THE PRIORITY OF COMMUNITY

The vision of the Sacred Revolution is shalom, and the top three priorities are gratitude, covenantal faithfulness, and community. We just finished an in-depth look at gratitude. An overview of covenantal faithfulness was presented in the chapter regarding shalom. Now it is time to look at the third priority, which is community.

Community is essential to the Sacred Revolution for three main reasons. The first reason is that we are biologically wired to need community. Humans are not meant to live in isolation. We require healthy social relationships and networks to thrive. The second reason is that for shalom to be realized, we need to feel that we belong and are connected in meaningful ways with those around us. The third reason is that, as we will see in this section, community is one of the primary ways we demonstrate our gratitude to God. Our practice of community out of gratitude is referred to as worship that is acceptable to God and shows reverence to God.

That community can function as an act of worship is a new concept for some. Taking up where we left off in the last chapter, we see in Hebrews how community and worship are tied together.

Recall Hebrews 12:28 stated, "let us give thanks, by which we offer to God an acceptable worship with reverence and awe." The passage will go on to list several examples of this acceptable worship such as mutual love, hospitality, caring for the members of the community that have been imprisoned, faithfulness in marriage, how we view money, caring for leaders of the community, and following Jesus. The whole section concludes with the phrase, "Do not neglect to do good and to share what you have, for such sacrifices are pleasing to God." The opening word "acceptable" and the closing word "pleasing" are both translated from the same root word in Greek. "Acceptable" and "pleasing" form bookends around the section that gives examples of what acceptable and pleasing look like to God. Notice that many of the examples are about community life. How we practice community is a form of acceptable worship of God.

Let's read the whole passage through. Following this I will break down the meaning of each section.

> Therefore, since we are receiving a kingdom that cannot be shaken, let us give thanks, by which we offer to God an acceptable worship with reverence and awe; for indeed our God is a consuming fire. Let mutual love continue. Do not neglect to show hospitality to strangers, for by doing that some have entertained angels without knowing it. Remember those who are in prison, as though you were in prison with them; those who are being tortured, as though you yourselves were being tortured. Let marriage be held in honor by all, and let the marriage bed be kept undefiled; for God will judge fornicators and adulterers. Keep your lives free from the love of money, and be content with what you have; for he has said, "I will never leave you or forsake you." So we can say with confidence, "The Lord is my helper; I will not be afraid. What can anyone do to me?" Remember your leaders, those who spoke the word of God to you; consider the outcome of their way of life, and imitate their faith. Jesus Christ is the same yesterday and today and forever. Do not be carried away by all kinds of strange teachings; for it is well for the heart to be strengthened by grace, not by regulations about food, which have not benefited those who observe them. We have an altar from which those who officiate in the tent have no right to eat. For the bodies of those animals whose blood is brought into the sanctuary by

the high priest as a sacrifice for sin are burned outside the camp. Therefore, Jesus also suffered outside the city gate in order to sanctify the people by his own blood. Let us then go to him outside the camp and bear the abuse he endured. For here we have no lasting city, but we are looking for the city that is to come. Through him, then, let us continually offer a sacrifice of praise to God, that is, the fruit of lips that confess his name. Do not neglect to do good and to share what you have, for such sacrifices are pleasing to God. (Hebrews 12:28-13:16)

Mutual Love

Let mutual love continue. (Hebrews 13:1)

The first admonition on the list is to practice love of one another and to do so in such a way that we would resemble siblings. The word translated here as "mutual love" is philadelphia in Greek which means "brotherly love." In Greek whenever you are referring to a mixed gender crowd it is always referred to in the masculine. To keep the concept gender neutral, the translators opted for "mutual love" over "brotherly love" which is correct, except it leaves the type of love undefined. We are called to practice a sibling style of love, which means that we are expected to share the strongest bond of love known in the ancient world. This is different from what modern Americans think of love. We are more apt to think of romantic love as the strongest bond. Understanding the difference between our definition of love and how love is assumed within the Bible is critical if we are going to fulfill this first and foundational call to practice mutual love.

We tend to think of love in primarily emotional terms, such as intense attraction or fond feelings for someone or something. Because of this, it can frustrate us that Jesus asks us to love people we do not naturally have affection for. The disconnect is that in the culture of Jesus' day love is not about emotion. Emotions may be a part of the experience of love in the biblical context, but love in the Bible has to do with solidarity or group attachment. The apostle Paul gives us a beautiful description of love that is often read at weddings. However, love is not described as an emotion, but as practices that bind a group together:

> Love is patient; love is kind; love is not envious or boastful or arrogant or rude. It does not insist on its own way; it is not irritable or resentful; it does not rejoice in wrongdoing, but rejoices in the truth. It bears all things, believes all things, hopes all things, endures all things. (1 Corinthians 13:4-7)

Paul is writing to a faith community that is struggling with division. He is encouraging them to see love as the most important of the spiritual gifts, and the proper practice of love will heal their divisions. Because love is a set of practices defining how we are expected to treat and respond to each other, we can understand how Jesus is able to ask us to have love for each other. Paul's list is not exhaustive of the full understanding of love, but it provides us with core concepts so we can have a starting point in learning how to practice love. It is important that we look a little closer at Paul's description of love because we have just learned that our gratitude to God is to be demonstrated in acts of worship that are pleasing to God, and the first example of pleasing worship is to continue in acts of love toward one another. Paul's admonitions can be grouped as such: how to show love, and how not to show love.

Patience

First on the list of how to show love is to be patient. Sometimes just taking the time to hear the whole story, or being understanding while someone is learning, can make all the difference. Our world is so fast-paced and hurried that we can find it hard to make time for others. Our time is a precious gift we can share with others. Taking time and being patient with others builds the bonds of community.

Kindness

The demonstration of kindness can be as simple as showing patience. Often it is our failure to be patient that causes us to be unkind. Notice each other with a smile or a wave. Help others to feel welcome and included. It does not take much on our part, but those little acts of kindness are vital for building community.

Both patience and kindness are connected to how we choose to perceive a given situation. We rarely know the motive or circumstances behind other people's actions. If we want to believe that others were acting deliberately to offend when stressful situations arise, we will be less willing to show patience or kindness. Our assumptions of others affect our willingness to demonstrate patience and kindness. If we make it a practice to assume the best in other's actions, patience and kindness will follow.

Truth

Next is rejoicing in truth. Truth is not always easy to hear or accept, let alone rejoice. To rejoice in truth means that we value learning the truth and acting on it over defending what has always been believed. This means that we have to be open to change, and the fact that we may have been wrong about something we believe in. This is not easy. When belief is challenged by new truth, and people are unwilling to accept the truth, this leads to divisions and attacks. If we have the patience to hear each other, and work through the differences of opinion with kindness, and with the goal of upholding the truth as best as we can understand it, then we can have a healthy community that is able to grow and change.

Bear, Believe, Hope, and Endure All Things

Paul concluded his list of positive traits of love with an admonition to bear, believe, hope, and endure all things. One of the primary benefits of living in community is the presence of others that can help in times of need. This means that you are required to help bear others' burdens. Additionally, we are choosing to believe the best in others, maintain a hopeful outlook, and commit to the hard but rewarding work of being community.

How amazing is it that what God expects as acts of worship is to practice love with one another? The sacrifice that God expects is not one of blood, but of doing away with the violence and selfishness within. It is this turmoil that breaks down community and God's vision of shalom.

Envy

Envy had a slightly different meaning in Paul's day. We tend to think of envy as wanting something that someone else has. How envy worked in the time of Jesus and Paul was as a means of correcting imbalance in a community's perception of honor. Envy is the emotion that others in the community feel toward someone who was raised above their honor status. We have seen how compliments can be used to socially shame others by drawing attention to someone's change in status. Envy works in a similar way, but may include more forceful actions or violence. For example, in Mark 15:10 Pilate was reasoning why Jesus was sent to him: "For he realized that it was out of jealousy that the chief priests had handed him over." The word translated as jealousy here is envy in the Greek. The arrest, beating, and crucifixion were defamation rituals designed to shame Jesus and take away his honor. Envy was a tool for maintaining community, to help prevent members from stepping out of line; however, it functions from the place of coercion rather than love, and it is resistant to learning and change. There is no place for envy in the Sacred Revolution and its communities.

Boastfulness, Arrogance, and Rude Behavior
The next three vices listed by Paul go together: boastfulness, arrogance, and rudeness—all symptoms of self-importance. These have no place in maintaining community. Boasting fails to recognize our place in the community. Arrogance fails to recognize the contributions of others. Rude behavior fails to recognize our interdependence on others. Each of these are symptoms of individualism and are summed up nicely by Paul's statement that love does not insist on its own way.

Irritability and Resentment
Irritability and resentment usually appear when frustrated with other people. Being self-aware of when frustration is controlling our behaviors will allow us to make a conscious effort to adjust our attitudes. When someone feels justified in acting irritated or resentful, it makes others feel unsafe in the community. We need to learn healthy ways to express our emotions if we want to have healthy community.

Wrongdoing
Finally, Paul warns about rejoicing in wrongdoing. Not only does this apply to not taking enjoyment from our own transgressions, but also from someone else's wrongs. Sometimes we want to live vicariously through others who do things that we would never do, such as acts of violence, sex, greed, or cruelty. Love is about doing what is right.

> The children of God and the children of the devil are revealed in this way: all who do not do what is right are not from God, nor are those who do not love their brothers and sisters. (1 John 3:10)

Living a Loving Life

The way of the Sacred Revolution is a way of doing, and not just about believing certain ideas about God or Jesus. To not live out our faith in tangible ways identifies us as a child of the devil—that is, as someone in opposition to the will of God. John tells us that you are recognized as a child of God when you do what is right and demonstrate love to our brothers and sisters. John continues:

> Those who say, "I love God," and hate their brothers or sisters, are liars; for those who do not love a brother or sister whom they have seen, cannot love God whom they have not seen. The commandment we have from him [Jesus] is this: those who love God must love their brothers and sisters also. (1 John 4:20-21)

Having love for one another is at the top of the list in these passages from John, Paul, and the letter to the Hebrews because it is essential. Your love of God is demonstrated in the love you show your neighbor. Nothing else is possible in discipleship without love. If the first and greatest command is to love God, the validity of our love of God is evaluated by our demonstration of love to our brothers and sisters in Christ. Jesus said that we even need to love our enemies; we cannot dehumanize our enemies to justify mistreating them. We need to see all people as made in God's image and not use their inexcusable behavior to justify a response from us that stoops to their level of behavior.

We need to feel safe within our faith community. Our current culture will respond to our resistance to their ways, sometimes by devastating means. At times like that you and I need to know that our brothers and sisters have our backs. We build that confidence in our community by our commitment to gathering together even when it is inconvenient. The practice of love when things are good builds the character and virtue needed to sustain the community through the hard times.

Do not miss the truly shocking reality this command creates. We have been made into a family! We have a place where we belong and are missed when we are away. How much is that worth? Some of us do not have biological family nearby, and some of us have biological family that does not act like family. Your participation in a community of faith may be more important to others in the community than you can ever imagine. Do not underestimate how important you are to our faith community. Our time and commitment to each other is worth more than anything in the world. Healthy and loving faith communities are what God intended for us. Truly healthy communities are hard to find because so few are willing to risk loving others. This is why practicing mutual/sibling love is at the top of the list defining acceptable worship to God.

A quote from Stanley Hauerwas in his book *In Good Company* speaks to the foundational importance of community. In fact, he refers to proper community practices as salvation:

> Salvation is being engrafted into practices that save us from those powers that would rule our lives making it impossible for us to truly worship God.

Being "engrafted into practices" is a way of speaking about entering into a community that is defined by certain ways of life. In this case, Stanley is referring to practices that allow us to successfully resist the powers of the Domination System. If we do not succeed in resisting, the Domination System will pull us into dependencies and obligations that prevent us from living in ways that are pleasing to God. These are the dependencies and obligations that we feel pulling us when we find it hard to have the time and energy to gather with our new family. The context of participating in a committed community of faith is needed both to be able to resist the Domination System and to offer acceptable worship to God. And as Stanley says, this is salvation.

Hospitality

> Do not neglect to show hospitality to strangers, for by doing that some have entertained angels without knowing it. (Hebrews 13:2)

Hospitality is another word we use a little differently from its use in biblical times. We tend to use hospitality as a way to describe having friends over or entertaining people. Rather, hospitality in the biblical world is a means by which strangers are transformed into either friends or foes. In the ancient world most places did not have hotels. Travelers and aliens were at the mercy of those that would welcome them. They would depend on the hospitality of others. Hospitality is the method by which a stranger becomes either a friend or an enemy. Hospitality is a test to see if the stranger can respect the community values. If they can, then they can become friends. If not, then they have identified themselves as enemies.

Because strangers are often viewed with suspicion, it is easy for them to become marginalized, abused, or scapegoats for local trouble. Our God has particular concern for the aliens, strangers, widows, orphans, and the oppressed in general. As the people of God, we are called to share the same concerns for those most at risk among us.

> When an alien resides with you in your land, you shall not oppress the alien. The alien who resides with you shall be to you as the citizen among you; you shall love the alien as yourself, for you were aliens in the land of Egypt: I am the Lord your God. (Leviticus 19:33-34)

The stranger is still at risk today, and followers of Jesus are called to show hospitality. One difference between modern times and the ancient world is that there are many places like hotels for strangers to stay. Because our neighborhoods are not a close network like they were in the ancient world, there is far more risk in inviting strangers into our homes—that means we need to be creative in how we practice hospitality. Here is another time that being part of a community is helpful, as our ability to work together to help is more than any one of us could accomplish alone.

Hospitality is the chance for the stranger to prove themselves a friend to the community. In our modern context, we tend to view the church as having responsibilities to the larger public—to care for anyone who falls through the cracks. The church has lost its identity as a distinct community and has become a volunteer department of the state. On the one hand, we are called to love our enemies, which may include helping with basic needs to the extent that we are able, but that is not hospitality. Caring for our enemies is our refusal to dehumanize them. It is to continue to show our essential solidarity with everyone because all people are made in the image of God, even if they have forgotten that fact. When we welcome the stranger into our community, they are welcome to stay if they prove to be a friend. If they prove to be an enemy, they are not welcome. Being a part of a Sacred Community is a reciprocal relationship based on a covenant and a commitment to be accountable to the covenant. The community has responsibilities to the members and the members have responsibilities to the community.

Whether someone is in or out of the community has to do with accountability. We are defined by making the intentional choice to follow Jesus and his way of life. What should we do if somebody wants to be a part of our community, but they do not share our core values? What if they are someone who is not interested in showing love to their enemy? A person who is not interested in practicing mutual concern for one another and accountability to each other?

Biblically, if someone refuses to participate in proper relationships, they are excluded from the community. The fact that excommunication has no place in many of our contemporary churches is an indictment on our understanding of the church. We love to quote Jesus when he says "if two or more are gathered in my name, I am there with them," but we fail to notice that this is said in the context of making decisions on excommunication.

> If another member of the church sins against you, go and point out the fault when the two of you are alone. If the member listens to you, you have regained that one. But if you are not listened to, take one or two others along with you so that every word may be confirmed by the evidence of two or three witnesses. If the member refuses to listen to them, tell it to the church. And if the offender refuses to listen even to the church, let such a one be to you as a gentile and a tax collector. Truly I tell you that whatever you bind on earth will be bound in heaven. And whatever you loose on earth will be loose in heaven. Again, truly I tell you if two of you agree on earth about anything you ask, it will be done for you by my Father in heaven. For where two or three are gathered in my name, there I am among them. (Matthew 18:15-20)

It may seem strange to discuss excommunication in a section on hospitality, but it is necessary to put hospitality in its proper context and importance. Hospitality and excommunication go hand-in-hand. Hospitality is not something you can offer to your friends or family. Nor can you offer hospitality to an enemy. Hospitality from a biblical perspective is the means whereby strangers are tested to see if they are friend or foe. If friend, we welcome them as such and offer fellowship. If an enemy, they have excluded themselves from the community, but we still show acts of mercy and love when the enemy is in true need.

This is why accountability is so important when you are talking about fellowship. As a Sacred Community, we are mutually striving to be like Jesus, to be disciples, to follow Jesus in his Sacred Revolution. We commit to holding each other accountable to our covenantal convictions because it is too easy to fail on our own and there is too much at stake.

The type of sin that Jesus is discussing in this passage from Matthew is not someone struggling to do what they know they should. A common example is the need to forgive someone who has wronged you. Forgiving can be hard to do even when you know you need to. The type of sin that Jesus is addressing is when someone rejects the values they have committed to. To use the example of needing to forgive someone who has wronged you, this sin would have moved past, "I am having trouble doing what I know I should," to "I don't care. I am no longer interested in being that kind of person."

Jesus counsels us to go to the offender to see if we can be reconciled. If they still do not want to be reconciled, we are to bring other people from the community to see if there is a way to work out the issue and move towards reconciliation. If their response is something like, "You know what? Screw you guys. I'm not interested in doing this, and I'm not going to do it. Don't come around asking me to take care of this anymore," then it has escalated into an issue that could divide the community and the community needs to address the issue.

When we begin our worship service, we have the "passing of the peace." This is the time for us to demonstrate that all are at peace with one another. If we are not, we stop right there because it is much more important to resolve whatever the issue is before we do anything else.

Without mutual love being the foundation that binds us all together, there is no discipleship, there is no moving forward. If we do not understand how to work out issues, how to reconcile them, or how to practice love with one another, then we are just fooling ourselves if we think we love God, or that we can go out and tell other people what they are supposed to do.

In the Sermon on the Mount Jesus says, "when you are offering your gift at the altar, if you remember that your brother or sister has something against you, leave your gift there before the altar and go; first be reconciled to your brother or sister, and then come and offer your gift" (Matthew 5:23-24).

All the aspects we think of regarding worship—whether we are talking about prayer, tithing, or even the service itself—are second to the issue of being reconciled with our brothers and sisters. It is that foundational. Our worship and witnesses are worthless if we are not a living example of a reconciled community.

The use of excommunication is not about kicking someone out. Excommunication is a formalization of the fact that someone has excluded themselves by rejecting the values the community is defined by. The hope of excommunication is that it will alert the one who is out of fellowship to how serious the situation is so that they might repent and come back.

In the Sacred Revolution salvation is being engrafted into the Sacred Community that is living out God's vision of shalom. That means that the issue of inclusion and exclusion are severe issues. This is why Jesus continues in Matthew 18:18 by saying, "Truly I tell you that whatever you bind on earth will be bound in heaven. And whatever you loose on earth will be loosed in heaven. Again, truly I tell you if two of you agree on earth about anything you ask, it will be done for you by my Father in heaven. For where two or three are gathered in my name, there I am among them."

The binding and loosing language is about inclusion and exclusion from the community with the corollary concern of salvation—the earth and heaven language. Because the stakes are so high, Jesus promises to be with his people in the midst of the difficult process of excommunication, even if there are only two or three gathered in his name. It is interesting how often this last verse is used about worship, but the context is the serious issue of excommunication. And we have to take this seriously. Because if the body does not respect itself, it will come completely undone.

But excommunication is not a tool to make sure there are only perfect people in the community. This is not about kicking people out that do not live up to our expectations. People will fail to be perfect all the time. The only time excommunication comes into play is when someone has demonstrated that they are no longer concerned about the community values. But for the rest of us who consistently fail to live up to the values we proclaim, the passage in Matthew continues:

> Then Peter came and said to him, "Lord, if another member of the church sins against me, how often should I forgive? As many as seven times?"
> (Matthew 18:21)

The tradition at the time that Peter asks this question was that you gave someone three chances. Peter is trying to be expansive. "As many as seven times?" That is over twice as many as the tradition.

> Jesus said to him, "Not seven times, but, I tell you, seventy-seven times." (Matthew 18:22)

Seventy-seven is not meant to be a specific number of times. The seventy-eighth time was not when you were freed from an obligation to forgive. This number comes from one of the stories in Genesis.

You may remember that Cain was one of the two sons born to Adam and Eve and that he killed his brother Abel. Cain's punishment is that he his banished (excommunicated), and is forced to wander the earth. Cain complains that anyone who finds him will want to kill him, to which God replies:

> Then the Lord said to him, "Not so! Whoever kills Cain will suffer a sevenfold vengeance." And the Lord put a mark on Cain, so that no one who came upon him would kill him. (Genesis 4:15)

The sixth generation from Cain is Lamech, who confesses to having hurt and then killed a young man (which might be in reference to Enoch, who dies at the "young" age of 365 years. When everybody else is living to nearly 1000, his life is cut short). Lamech then says: If Cain is avenged sevenfold, truly Lamech seventy-sevenfold (Genesis 4:24). So Jesus is taking this statement of vengeance, and turning it around to use it as a statement about forgiveness. Practicing forgiveness is essential in Sacred Communities. Without the clear understanding that we are a community that forgives, people will seek to hide their failures and become judgmental toward others' failures.

The reason we are spending any time on excommunication is because it sheds light on the question of hospitality. A Sacred Community is not—as it is sometimes described by others—a "doormat" for people to walk all over. There is a definition to the community that defines who we are and what we do, and we hold each other accountable to those values. If someone is refusing to be a part of our community and to be accountable to discipleship, then they are not considered part of the community. We still treat them with the utmost respect. We recognize them as someone made in the image of God. But people are not free to come in and reap whatever kind of havoc they want within a Sacred Community. This explains the hard part of hospitality: what we do with strangers that prove to be a foe.

Now let's look at the second half of this verse:

> Do not neglect to show hospitality to strangers, for by doing that some have entertained angels without knowing it. (Hebrews 13:2)

I want to share with you a story I heard recently during a sermon. It is called The Rabbi's Gift and was written by Friar Francis Dorff, O. Praem. It takes place in New York, where there is increasing trouble within a monastery. Some of the monks lacked a sense of urgency and purpose. Some were asking what they were doing and why. The monks had become apathetic, and strife was creeping in.

People in the community used to attend different events and worship services the monastery offered, but were starting to stay away because they noticed that something had changed. This only intensified the questioning and apathy of the monks.

One of the head monks was in town when he ran into a rabbi. For some reason, the monk felt like he could share his concerns about the monastery with the rabbi. The monk then asked the rabbi, "Do you have any ideas about what we can do to turn things around?" The rabbi said, "I have no idea. But I do have this sense—that one of you at the monastery is the long awaited Messiah." Then the rabbi left.

The monk was stunned. Why would the rabbi say this? The monk thought about it and he said to himself, "I know it's not me." He considered some of his brothers at the monastery, and concluded that it could be a number of them. He wondered if he would be able to recognize the Messiah.

He went back and told his fellow monks what had happened. The monks pondered what it could mean. Over time, the monks changed how they were relating to one another because in the back of everyone's mind was the question, could that brother be the one? None of them wished to behave badly in front of the Messiah.

The fellowship at the monastery gradually transformed. The surrounding community recognized that something different was going on. The monks acted and behaved in a more determined, faithful manner, and this attracted others to them. Others wanted to be a part of something good. The whole situation had turned around because they looked at each with kindness rather than doubt and negativity. By seeing others worthy of hospitality, it did not matter who they were—the messiah or a stranger. I think this is what is happening in our passage in Hebrews: "some have entertained angels without knowing it."

A similar concept was used by Mother Teresa when she explained how she had the motivation to engage with the very poorest-of-the-poor. She said that the poor were "Jesus in a distressing disguise." So the possibility of entertaining angels should govern how we think about people we do not know. How might that transform our view of a stranger if we put that into practice, over the fear that the media wants to pump into our heads? Imagine how you might treat people differently if you worked at seeing others as Jesus in disguise or as an angel.

We do not want to bypass the process of hospitality and just assume that strangers intend us harm. We are especially at risk of jumping to assumptions when we see the tensions heating up over border issues and how foreigners and minorities are presented in the media.

But think about this: everyone is more than they appear. Everyone is made in the image of God! When I look at my own life I ask myself, how can that be? There are so many areas of my life that are broken it seems impossible that I am somehow the image of God. I imagine it is just as hard for you to consider this in your own life. And as we look at others it can be hard to believe it about them as well.

Perhaps we are all in a distressing disguise and we need to look through it to see what God sees, that we are someone God cares for, even when everyone else has given up. We are someone that Jesus faced torture and death for so that we might be redeemed. We need to see ourselves as someone precious to God.

Recognizing the Image of God in all people will transform how you see the world. As more of us commit to seeing the Image of God in everyone, the world itself will be transformed. Remember to show hospitality to the stranger, for in doing so some have entertained angels and did not know it.

Here is a recap of what we have learned about acceptable or pleasing worship. We are called to first practice a brotherly/sisterly love for one another. And for those who we do not know, the stranger, do not marginalize them, but rather offer hospitality in the hopes that they will become a part of the community.

Supporting Fellow Resisters

> Remember those who are in prison, as though you were in prison with them; those who are being tortured, as though you yourselves were being tortured.
> (Hebrews 13:3)

This verse is referring to brothers and sisters suffering for the faith. We know this is the case because the same topic is brought up earlier in chapter ten of Hebrews:

> But recall those earlier days when, after you had been enlightened, you endured a hard struggle with sufferings, sometimes being publicly exposed to abuse

and persecution, and sometimes being partners with those so treated. For you had compassion for those who were in prison, and you cheerfully accepted the plundering of your possessions, knowing that you yourselves possessed something better and more lasting. (Hebrews 10:32-34)

The author of Hebrews is reminding his audience of their endurance of a past situation, to encourage them to endure current circumstances. He brings up their initial conversion to the faith—their enlightenment—so that they can reflect on where they came from and who they were before following Jesus in the way of true humanity. Their transformation of life cost them dearly.

What kind of public abuse did they face? To begin with, there was the problem of groceries. To understand this, you have to understand a little bit about how ancient cities work. Every city has its patron deity. A patron deity was the god responsible for the well-being and protection of the city and its people. It is an expected part of everyone's civic responsibility to participate in the cultic celebrations and worship of the local deity. Keeping the local god happy is how the people of a city hoped to prevent things like famine, war, and pestilence. For the followers of Jesus, worshiping the local deity was problematic because the disciples believed that there is only one God and to worship false gods would be disrespectful to God. Followers of Jesus cannot worship, or bow down to, or serve any of the false gods.

By not participating in civic duties of worship, followers of Jesus invited suspicion on themselves. The other citizens viewed the followers of Jesus as atheists because they did not participate in sacrifices to the local god. The community addressed by the letter to the Hebrews ran the risk of being shunned and being excluded by the other citizens out of fear, because if anything went wrong in the city they would be blamed. The city officials would be looking at followers of

Jesus because they refused to pay proper respect to the local deity. The possible offense to the gods was too great of a threat to the city for the locals to ignore the nonparticipation of the Jesus followers. At the very least, locals would keep their distance to avoid being viewed as guilty by association. Additionally, the main source of meat in the market was from animals sacrificed to gods during the civic worship. By not participating in the sacrifices, the Jesus followers would find it hard to even have access to meat.

Think about how much pressure the need for basic resources would put on you to conform, to just go along with what everyone else was doing, even if you did not believe it. The main threat to the earliest followers was not the threat of violence, it was the threat of exclusion. It was the loss of social standing and the loss of material comforts that most others had access to. Sometimes local hostility would escalate to widespread persecution.

The beginning of the Christian movement was mostly made up of Jews, and most of the Gentile world viewed Christianity as a Jewish sect. Around 49 AD, the Emperor Claudius issued an edict expelling the Jews from Rome. The book of Acts of the Apostles makes reference to this event when describing a couple that Paul met coming from Rome:

> A Jew named Aquila, a native of Pontus, who had recently come from Italy with his wife Priscilla, because Claudius had ordered all Jews to leave Rome.
> (Acts 18:2)

Suetonius was a Roman historian that lived from 69 AD to 122AD. In his work, "Lives of the Twelve Caesars," he makes mention of this event and helps to explain why it happened:

> Since the Jews constantly made disturbances at the instigation of Chrestus, he [Emperor Claudius] expelled

them from Rome. (Suetonius, Lives of the Twelve Caesars, Divus Claudius 25)

The name "Chrestus" is believed to be a Latin version of Christos, the Greek word for Christ. It is possible that in Rome the Jews were fighting among themselves about Jesus, or Jesus-following Jews were causing some kind of disruption with the Gentiles. In either case, Claudius expelled all Jews from Rome. Many scholars believe this is the event mentioned in Hebrews that caused public shame and allowed them to be despoiled of their possessions. The Gentile Christians were not required to leave Rome, yet the author of Hebrews suggest that at least some of the Gentile Christians continued to show solidarity with their exiled brothers and sisters. Later, the Apostle Paul would write a letter to the Romans that is addressing the reintegration of the Jewish Christians into the Gentile Christian church in Rome after the death of Claudius.

When considering what constitutes acceptable or pleasing worship to God, Hebrews calls us to continue to practice solidarity when our brothers and sisters suffer as a result of their resistance to the Domination System. This is part of our struggle for faithfulness to the calling of true humanity. It is our solidarity, or love, that enables us to practice resistance to the Domination System.

Our culture fights to maintain its way of life through sanctioning competing alternatives, just as all cultures do. The mere suggestion of alternatives is often met with violent emotional outrage and a desire to excommunicate. This is behind the sentiment, "America, love it or leave it!" It does not take long for the phrase to come up when someone challenges or questions some aspect of the American way of life. Our culture is increasingly defined by our free market capitalism and depends on an unending cycle of consumption. With this in mind, you can bet that your participation in the Sacred Revolution will be met with pushback from people embedded in our dominant culture.

Specifically, following Jesus in the Sacred Revolution comes with economic practices that challenge free market capitalism. These practices can range from refusing to make a profit by investing in companies engaged in practices we would not personally do, to working for more sustainable ways of living in order to stop the constant cycle of consumption of nonrenewable resources. Practices like these will bar us from experiencing all that our culture has to offer regarding material well-being. You will experience ridicule for your ideas and pressure to conform to the way that everyone else lives. If your protest and resistance become too public, you may even experience prison, or at least labeling designed to discredit your action in the public eye.

Are you prepared for this level of resisting? Very few of us could stand alone against the wall of pressure to conform. This is why the community of love is vital to our existence and faithfulness in the Sacred Revolution.

Fidelity

> Let marriage be held in honor by all, and let the marriage bed be kept undefiled; for God will judge fornicators and adulterers. (Hebrews 13:4)

Nothing will destroy a community as quickly as infidelity or irresponsible sexual activity. Broken marriages, unwanted pregnancies, and crushed hearts (as a result of too much intimacy without commitment), are poison to any kind of community. Because of this, sex within a sacred community is not a private matter. How we live our lives and the choices we make have a profound impact on all the rest of us.

We live in a culture that promotes and celebrates the individual. We do not like the idea that we are responsible to, or connected to, others. We want to be free to make whatever decisions we want for ourselves. But here is the truth: there is no independence for anyone, only the illusion of independence. Those that seem like they have the most autonomy in our culture (rock stars, billionaire CEOs, etc.), are still dependent on millions of people buying their products or services. And the ability for millions to buy stuff is only possible if everyone is participating in a common economic system.

In days gone by our interdependence was more obvious. We had face-to-face interaction with our customers. If someone got pregnant out of wedlock, it was not as easy to get rid of it and your family and community were going to be impacted. If a fire broke out, the community had to work together to prevent the town from burning down, and then the community would come together to help rebuild; that was the insurance that others would help you if your place burned.

Today we can sell stuff to people on the Internet and never meet them. Kids can get an abortion without their parents even knowing about it. We have insurance for everything so that we do not need to have networks of friends and neighbors to help. We are all still interdependent through our participation in the government and economic system, but now that interconnectedness is anonymous. We do not know, nor are we accountable to, those we are connected with. This anonymity is what give us the illusion of autonomy.

Anonymity brings out different behavior in people. You could drop a Playboy magazine in a small church where everyone knows each other, and the young men will avoid that magazine like it was the plague. But the chances are much higher that those same boys would eagerly grab the magazine as a treasure if they came across it on the sidewalk in a part of town where no one knew them. Anonymity enables financial fraud, unjust policies, racism, violence, and basically the worst in human behavior. When we recognize our connectedness to others, and when we are accountable to them for our actions, we treat each other better.

In our autonomy obsessed society, we think there is a choice to be made between being an individual and being part of a group. But there is no choice, we are all connected and our actions do impact others. The only choice to be made is, which system do you want to be connected to? Do you want to be connected to a community committed to becoming truly human and holding each other accountable to that goal, or do you want to be dependent on an anonymous and impersonal system that uses propaganda, debt, and fear to get you to make "free" choices for the system's benefit?

The more we have the experience of being an individual, the more we are vulnerable to being controlled by the system. The Domination System's basic plan is to create, through education and media, consumers that are never satisfied and are consequently in debt. It wants to create consumers who cannot stop working long enough to question why they are doing what they are doing, and so cannot organize any kind of resistance. To be individualized is to be divided. Individualism is a false desire (because it is impossible and only an illusion), designed to make you controllable. At the same time, this false desire makes you believe that accountable community is the worst possible social arrangement. The Domination System is a system that creates classes of haves and have-nots. A system that depends on inequality. A system that will force you to ignore the brutality and inhumanity it inflicts on others.

The focus on community over the individual is not to dismiss the uniqueness of gifts and personality that each of us has. We want to celebrate our uniqueness while acknowledging our interconnectedness. The Sacred Revolution is a way of life that we voluntarily enter into. The way of life we live in the Sacred Revolution defines us as a certain kind of people. We are a people that do not use others as objects to feed our desires at their expense. We are a people that do not engage in creating intimate bonds with others without the stability of commitment in place first. And we are a people that respect the commitments that we and others make.

It is vital that someone make the choice to adopt this way of life. If we try to force our way of life on others, we transform our way of life into coercion and brutality. We become a new system of domination. Yes, the Sacred Revolution comes with some radical life changes, but those changes should come about because someone can see how these practices bring forth true humanity and protect against dehumanizing practices. Accountability and interdependence in the faith community are necessary for this way of life.

To prevent the formation of our communities of resistance, the Domination System engages in widespread propaganda aimed at convincing us to fear dependence on community and to increase our desired autonomy; however, we know that autonomy is an illusion. The Domination System's lure away from dependence on a community is the acquisition of wealth. Wealth in our culture allows one to be free of accountability and exchanges personal interconnectedness for anonymous connections. Wealth is the next topic the author of Hebrews addresses.

Wealth

> Keep your lives free from the love of money, and be content with what you have; for he has said, "I will never leave you or forsake you." So we can say with confidence, "The Lord is my helper; I will not be afraid. What can anyone do to me?" (Hebrews 13:5-6)

When we looked at the section on supporting resisters, we saw that part of our call to worship includes maintaining solidarity with our brothers and sisters that are suffering or have lost possessions as a result of their living in faithfulness to Jesus. Our loss of possessions, or even our exclusion from financial systems, can be a powerful temptation to break from the Sacred Revolution. These verses counsel us against showing solidarity (love) with money.

I have discussed wealth at length in the section on shalom. Here I would like to look at the strategy presented for having a life free from the love of money—contentment. The logic is easy enough to follow: if I am content with what I have and where I am at in my life, then I will not be tempted to chase after money to better my situation. But contentment can lead to inaction. What would ever change if we all decided we are content?

When the author of Hebrews suggests that we adopt contentment as a desired mental state, it brings two important questions to mind. First, what if there is a real need to change a situation? Should we be content in the face of political oppression or corporate pollution, for example? Second, what if we cannot meet some of our basic needs like food or shelter? Should we be content if we do not have enough food for our kids to eat?

It would appear that promoting contentment would be a strategy for any system that does not want change—systems that do not want you to ask questions that could inspire change, especially questions about the distribution of goods. When we experience discontentment it is because we are comparing our situation to that of others.

Contentment cannot be universal in the Domination System because it depends on endless consumption by consumers in a never-ending quest for more; nevertheless, there are areas of our lives that we are told to be content with:

1.   We should be content with our political and economic system. We are told that our system represents the highest and noblest form of government in human history. We are

warned that those who seek change at this level will bring the whole system down and we will find ourselves in a dangerous and lawless dystopian world. **Response**: While it can be argued that our current political and economic systems are the best to date in many respects, that does not mean it is perfect or that there is not serious need to continue to change for the better.

2.   We should be content with inequality. We are taught that what makes our system great is that it does not fight against human nature. It embraces the pursuit of self-interest as the only true motivation. The pursuit of self-interest will result in some having more than others, but we are told that this is a result of some working harder than others. We are warned that those who question inequality want to drag us to an oppressive form of government like Socialism or Marxism. **Response**: While we need to honor those who work hard, they need to be rewarded in a way that is sustainable and promotes the common good. It must also be acknowledged that those with more are not just a result of having worked hard. We inherit much in this world from where we are born, who our parents are, our access to education and social networks, cultural prejudice, and natural physical ability. In fact, this lottery of birth will have the largest impact on what we have before working hard is ever factored in. The majority of people in this world will never be rewarded in proportion to their efforts.

3.   We should be content with the over consumption of natural resources and the pollution of the environment to continue economic development. We are told to ignore the overwhelming majority of scientists who all point to irreversible damage being done to our ecological system by our actions. **Response**: We need to radically change our economic system and political policies to avert a crisis that threatens all life on earth. The vested interests of private energy corporations are a powerful incentive to maintain the status quo and make it almost impossible to change.

Even though contentment is important to the Domination System, it has a strategic use rather than universal application. This is also true in how contentment is applied in the Sacred Revolution. The specific use of contentment in this passage, "Keep your lives free from the love of money, and be content with what you have;" is to counter the temptation to seek after wealth as a means of security. Contentment in this context is not used as a strategy to prevent social change, or working to achieve one's basic needs.

The people of God are reassured that they will not be abandoned, "for he has said, 'I will never leave you or forsake you.'" This quote is a general restatement of various promises from God in the Hebrew Scriptures rather than an exact quote. Remember that the New Testament did not exist for the first followers of Jesus. The Hebrew Scriptures were their Bible.

That God will be with them calls for a response from the community, "So we can say with confidence". Confidence, as used in this verse, also refers to courage. "The Lord is my helper; I will not be afraid. What can anyone do to me?" That God is with the community calls for a courageous response in the face of persecution from others who would take their possessions or otherwise threaten them. This quote is a congregational response of praise from Psalm 118:6.

In Hebrews 13:5-6, contentment is about courageously continuing in the way of God without fear rather than trusting in wealth for salvation. Worship that is acceptable and pleasing to God will not lead to the seeking of wealth as a means to achieve security or independence.

Leaders

Remember your leaders, those who spoke the word of God to you; consider the outcome of their way of life, and imitate their faith. Jesus Christ is the same yesterday and today and forever. (Hebrews 13:7-8)

What is a leader of the Sacred Revolution? Three important parts of being a leader are mentioned here: speaking the word of God, living as an example, and the evaluation of their teaching and life by the witness of Jesus. Keep in mind that all of these attributes apply to all of us. The distinction for our leaders is that within our community they have been recognized as having additional gifts of correctly discerning the will of God and then sharing what they have learned in understandable and motivational ways with the rest of us. Their discernment is not to be the result of special revelation that only they can reveal; rather, we are to evaluate everything by the witness of Jesus, who does not change. It is their ability to interpret the historical and cultural witness of Jesus in reliable ways that are recognized. What will be unique, is the leader's vision for how the witness of Jesus gets lived out in our particular time and place.

I would like to bring up one of the attributes for leaders within the community that Jesus mentions directly. This comes from Matthew 20:24-28. In this passage we overhear a disagreement between the disciples as two of them have requested positions of leadership in their community:

> When the ten heard it, they were angry with the two brothers. But Jesus called them to him and said, "You know that the rulers of the Gentiles lord it over them, and their great ones are tyrants over them. It will not be so among you; but whoever wishes to be great among you must be your servant, and whoever wishes to be first among you must be your slave; just as the Son of Man came not to be served but to serve, and to give his life a ransom for many." (Matthew 20:24-28)

Leadership in the Sacred Revolution is not about power or coercion. It is about encouragement and teaching, community building and vision casting, serving and participation. Again, the ways of leadership are to imitate the ways of Jesus, just as we all are expected to do as his followers. As we look at these attributes of our leaders, remember that they apply to all of us.

Firstly we are called to remember. We are not to forget or take for granted. This applies to previous leaders that have died or were called to new locations, as well as our current leaders. As leaders look out for the needs of our community, they run the risk of being overlooked themselves. Our leaders are just people like you or me, with all the same challenges of faithfulness to Jesus that all people face. Remember that it was through their labor of sharing life with us that we have received the word of God, and our lives have been transformed!

You may have heard the phrase, "faith is caught not taught," or, "people don't care how much you know until they know how much you care." This is certainly true of the Sacred Revolution. Our leaders are not supposed to just talk the talk, but to, as the saying goes, walk the walk. We are called to imitate the life of Jesus and the life of his faithful followers. We learn from other followers what discipleship looks like. Just hearing about Jesus or learning religious concepts does not translate easily into daily action for most people. We learn best by observing and imitating.

The importance of disciples actually living like Jesus serves another crucial role. This is how someone from outside or new to the faith evaluates the legitimacy of the faith. People do not have the patience for playing games or hypocrisy. They want to know that there is real power to transform their life into a life of significance. They want to know that there is a real alternative to the brutality and meaninglessness they currently live with. If the followers they know do not witness to the truthfulness of the faith by living

143

it out, they will not give the faith the time of day. Would you? The Sacred Revolution can never be simply an intellectual pursuit, it must be a tangible way of life modeled by its leaders and followers alike.

This does not mean that our leaders are perfect. We learn just as much, if not more, by how they handle their failures. We do them and ourselves a disservice if we place them on a pedestal expecting them to be something that we are not. Placing someone on a pedestal is a way to defer your responsibility for discipleship. We have a tendency to lift up our leaders and hold them to the standard while forgetting that we are also called to meet that same standard. We all stand equally before God. We most certainly need to practice accountability with our leaders, but that accountability extends to everyone in the community.

Offering acceptable and pleasing worship to God will include the recognition of leaders that are committed to shaping us into a community that lives like Jesus. It will involve us remembering our leaders and their labor on our behalf, and will include the practice of accountability to the way of Jesus amongst us all.

Following Jesus Out

> Do not be carried away by all kinds of strange teachings; for it is well for the heart to be strengthened by grace, not by regulations about food, which have not benefited those who observe them. We have an altar from which those who officiate in the tent have no right to eat. For the bodies of those animals whose blood is brought into the sanctuary by the high priest as a sacrifice for sin are burned outside the camp. Therefore, Jesus also suffered outside the city gate in order to sanctify the people by his own blood. Let us then go to him outside the camp and bear the abuse he endured. For here we have no

lasting city, but we are looking for the city that is to come. (Hebrews 13:9-14)

When we read this passage, we realize two things: we are listening in on the middle of a long conversation, and second, this comes from a very different culture than we live in. If the above passage sounds strange to you and you are not sure what to make of it, you are not alone. I will help you to understand the basic point that is being made.

We are presented with a contrast from which to choose. On one side there are regulations about food, an altar from which food cannot be eaten, and sacrifice for sin of which the body of the victims need to be brought outside the camp. This is described as a strange teaching, and of no benefit to those who observe it. The author is using imagery from Israel's past when they worshiped in a tabernacle (or tent). By doing so, it refers to the temple system from its foundation. The whole temple/palace complex is presented in a negative light and contrasts the grace, or gift, received from Jesus. The other choice is to follow Jesus out of the camp, out of the temple and palace. Jesus is presented as a victim of the temple/palace complex and his body is brought outside the city. It is outside the complex that Jesus' death works to sanctify people. This is no small matter and the ramifications will be explored in future volumes of this series. So what do we do with this information now? How do we apply this verse to offering acceptable and pleasing worship?

The religion of the Domination System will try to domesticate the Sacred Revolution by institutionalizing and regulating access to God. A temple literally is trying to put God in a box, and regulate access through a priestly class. They will quietly redefine the faith until it becomes a tool of support for the Domination System. It is at this point that we need to follow Jesus out. We need to be willing to suffer the abuse that he suffered in order to make a way for true humanity. What was once the dumping ground for the used carcasses of the sacrificial victims of the temple/palace complex becomes the meeting place for God's people. The food that could not be eaten has become the thanksgiving (Eucharist) meal that sustains our community outside the city. We are content to be outside the city (kingdom/empire) because we are waiting and working for another. Our willingness to follow Jesus out, even though it may cost us, is how we offer acceptable and pleasing worship to God.

Honor

> Through him, then, let us continually offer a sacrifice of praise to God, that is, the fruit of lips that confess his name. (Hebrews 13:15)

Understanding Sacrifice

Sacrifice is a technical term that describes the ceremonial transformation of an object from having a status of profane to a new status of sacred. That is the definition, now let me break that down so it is more understandable.

The Sacred Revolution views everything from the perspective of belonging. Belonging is similar to ownership but goes beyond mere possession and looks to attributes of the object that show where the object belongs. In particular, there is the question of belonging to God. This is why the question of attributes comes into play. God technically owns everything as creator, but we recognize objects as belonging to God when they possess attributes that reflect the attributes of God. When something belongs to God, we refer to them as holy or sacred. Holy and sacred are two different ways to describe something that belongs to God because it possesses attributes reflective of God.

Items that do not belong to God are referred to as common. Another traditional word for common is profane. In Latin, the word is vulgar. So originally profane and vulgar meant common or everyday. Vulgar or profane language simply means the language of common people. Sacrifice is how something changes its status from common (or profane) to sacred (or holy). Another word for sacrifice is sanctification.

Before we look at how this transformation happens, let's review the terms we have looked at so far. These words have typically had complex theological definitions that make it harder for people to understand. By helping you to grasp how these words work, I hope to show you how simple they actually are to understand.

What is something that is common/profane/vulgar? It is something that does not belong to God by reason of not having God-like attributes. For example, language that is used to belittle, abuse, or hurt someone does not represent attributes of God so it is considered common, profane, or vulgar language. But something can be common without being bad. When a culture has two languages, one for the elite and another for everyone else, the languages are functioning as a control technique to hide the elite's activities from those of lower class and to help identify what class someone belongs to by the language or accent they use. What is happening here is the reference for belonging has changed from God to the elite. What is common is what lacks attributes of the elite. In this case, we may find God at work in what is common or profane in relation to the elite. Jesus came as a commoner and not through the system of the elite, either the political or religious. At one point, the main language of the people was Latin but the Bible was preserved in the Greek language making the Bible inaccessible to most people. When the Bible was translated into Latin making it more accessible, it was referred to as the vulgar or vulgate translation. Common and profane and vulgar are ways of grouping things, periods of time, or people as not belonging to some group, individual, or God by reason of their attributes not matching. Jesus was profane to the political and religious system of his day because he did not behave like them, his attributes did not match. On the other hand, Jesus was not profane to God because Jesus represented God in his actions and teaching. Jesus' attributes reflected God's attributes. Therefore, Jesus belonged to God.

Sacred and holy are words we use to describe belonging. When things, periods of time, or people reflect attributes of God, they demonstrate that they belong to God and we call them holy or sacred. A sacred person is called a saint. All disciples of Jesus who are striving to look like Jesus in their actions are called saints. This does not mean that they are perfect, only that they have been set apart, or committed their lives to be disciples. Periods of time that are set apart for a purpose related to God are called holy. For example, we are called to remember the Sabbath day and to keep it holy. We keep it holy by participating within that time in a way that reflects God's attributes for that day. The same is true for things or places. If they are used in such a way that their use reflects attributes of God, then it is called holy. To help remember this concept you might think of holy as "wholly" or completely belonging to someone—not simply because someone owns it, but because the object reflects the attributes of the one it belongs to.

So this leaves us with the question, how does something move from being profane to holy? Status transformation is officiated by someone authorized for the task. We have examples of this throughout our society. When two individuals transform their status from single to married there is a ceremony which has an officiant who declares the transformation is valid and binding. When someone graduates from being a student to being a doctor, there is a ceremony and an officiant. Even with simple ownership transformation there is a sales clerk that is authorized to transfer the status of ownership after a financial ceremony (transaction).

Often there is a transition period in which the person or thing is no longer profane but not yet holy. A graduate student from medical school is no longer a lay-person, but they are not yet a doctor. This space is called a liminal space. Liminal space can also be seen when someone is engaged, as it is the space between them being single and married. When someone wants to enter the Sacred Revolution they enter into a period of training, traditionally called a catechism, and they are known as a catechumen. They are no longer an interested observer, but they have not yet made the final commitment to the covenant. The transition of status from a citizen of the Domination System to a Sacred Revolutionary (saint) involves the commitment of the individual to enter into the catechism (the liminal space), followed by the final commitment to the way of Jesus. This final commitment is demonstrated in a ceremony of baptism, officiated by a minister of the community. So sacrifice is the transition from profane to sacred.

Now that we have a better understanding of sacrifice we can look at what it means to offer a sacrifice of praise to God. A sacrifice of praise is language that has been transformed from common to holy as it is put to the service of God. By confessing the name (or attributes) of God, we increase God's honor, which is another way of saying God's reputation. This sacred language happens in two ways: when we testify to the faithfulness of God in our life to others, and in the worship service.

The Worship Service

The worship service is a community honoring of God's name and a proclamation that God is the one true Lord. This makes the worship service a demonstration of an alternative political allegiance. The seriousness of this act is why being allowed to participate in the full worship service within the Sacred Community is the final step of initiation into the Sacred Revolution. To invite others, who do not understand what they are doing, to participate in such a subversive act is irresponsible.

Because the worship service is a pledge and demonstration of allegiance, it is primarily an action we perform to and for God. This means the current debates about worship styles within various churches are misdirected. The main issue behind the use of different worship styles has been the personal preference of the participants; that is, we are asking the question of how can we make the service more appealing to a particular demographic. But does that make sense given that the worship service is intended for God? Should we not rather ask, "what kind of worship does God desire?" It is exactly the question of what constitutes acceptable worship that this passage in Hebrews has been addressing.

A Life Made Sacred

> Do not neglect to do good and to share what you have, for such sacrifices are pleasing to God. (Hebrews 13:16)

This section of scripture ends where we began by stating what is pleasing to God. The word for "pleasing" here is the same Greek word for "acceptable" that was used in verse 12:28. "Acceptable" and "pleasing" form bookends around this teaching that give us direction in how to properly worship God. The answer is both simple and amazing. Worship that is acceptable and pleasing to God consists of loving and caring for people that are made in God's image. This adds a new dimension and significance to anything from everyday actions like doing the dishes, to helping a stranger by offering some change. Whatever we do, if it involves loving and caring for others, will be pleasing acts of worship to God. Your life has been made sacred. Everything you do matters. Let's begin the Sacred Revolution together!

Part Four

Practices

"In the same way, let your light shine before others, so that they may see your good works and give glory to your Father in heaven."

- Jesus

RESISTING ANTI-REVOLUTION TACTICS

There are established programs of social control in place to prevent revolutions. The purpose of these programs is to uphold the established order by either making it too difficult to attempt change, or making it impossible to imagine a different way of life is possible. Understanding how these social controls work is the only way you can begin to resist them. You and everyone you know are affected. Breaking free of these anti-revolutionary controls is essential so that you can think clearly. You cannot serve God properly if your mind, thoughts, and will are controlled by others through these programs of social control.

Dependency is foundational to the Domination System. The more you are dependent on the system, the less likely you are to resist the way things are. To maintain the "basic" level of living, most people have to work 50–70 hours per week at jobs that are unfulfilling. More often than not, both spouses have to work so our children are raised primarily in daycare and school. After sleep, travel, and taking care of the house, we are lucky if we have 25% of our time for ourselves. Even those that appear to have the most freedom are dependent on the economic system which, in turn, is dependent on everything else connected to it. We have all seen how quickly that "freedom" disappears if something tweaks the system. The next thing you know, the government is bailing out institutions considered "too big to fail." A famous rock star or the CEO of a large multinational corporation are still dependent on masses of people exercising their "freedom" to buy their product. What makes this system seem like people have freedom is the emphasis on consumerism and autonomy.

Making choices as a consumer feels like freedom, but we are becoming more and more limited in any real choice in what we consume. Goods and services are owned and supplied by fewer mom-and-pop type stores, as they cannot compete with massive corporations. How many of the items you consume during the year come from a local resource and are made by local workers? It is becoming almost impossible to find anything that is 100% from the United States and made by Americans, let alone in your state or city. This global economic system is designed around specialization. When all the players specialize in just one part of the process, then everyone becomes dependent on that system because we no longer have the ability for local sustainability. At this point, the powers-that-be call all the shots and we do not have any real choice. We get to choose between the red or blue box, but we are still getting a box.

Even though we have become tangled up in this system of dependency, we still have the illusion of being autonomous, and that we are individuals independent of all others. The desire for autonomy and individualism is carefully crafted in the system. Real individualism and autonomy are impossible—we are all connected in innumerable ways. The only way to create the illusion of independence is to replace the dependence on others with dependence on the system. Now the social security, public works, and even the very economic basis of the system only work because we are all connected to it. This is why autonomy is an illusion. We are all still connected to each other, but now the connection is anonymous rather than face-to-face. The consequence of this anonymous connection is that people no longer have accountability to those they are connected to. But most importantly, our desire to be autonomous keeps us individualized and, therefore, weak.

Your path to resistance will consist of two main tasks:

1.   Identify and resist the tactics used to create dependence on the established order.

2. Become dependent on an alternative social group (a Sacred Community) in which new practices will free your mind for broader considerations of life in the world and God.

Let's explore four main tactics used to create dependency on the Domination System, and look at some tools of resistance you can begin to use right now. Remember, the system is an expert with enormous influence and resources. It will be hard to break free from its hold on your life. Take courage from your brother and sister revolutionaries and remember what is at stake. We have been called to demonstrate to the world that another way is possible and that the way of competition, greed, and brutality is not the only option. The world is starving for the way of Jesus, but they do not have enough examples of what that is supposed to look like. Too few Christians live the life Jesus invites us to live. If you and I do not show the world how it is done, then who will?

The First Anti-Revolution Tactic: Debt

One thing the Domination System does well is shape your desire; your desire for a lifestyle, for types of relationships, and for an endless list of consumer products. Consistent images found in stories, the news, on television, in movies, magazines, and public social spaces create a sense that this is the way things are, should be, and always have been. The heroes and trendsetters of our culture all uphold the image. Storefronts and malls all invite you to participate in the American dream. Easy credit and long term loans make it possible for you to obtain the objects of your manufactured desire. You can appear to live like the successful, but it is all financed.

The idea that you need more than you do starts from your earliest years. The commercials during children's television shows and the products provided by corporations to underfunded schools work to establish a brand identity as soon as possible in children. Billions of dollars are spent on teams of marketers and child psychologists to develop the most effective use of color, motion, and word combinations so that kids can effectively nag their parents into buying must-have desires. These desires have been carefully crafted—not by our children, but by the interests of the institutions and corporations that can reach them.

Need manipulation occurs for every age group. Those of us who are unaware of the fact that we are being spoon-fed do not stand a chance at resisting. The amount of resources and effort used to shape desire is nearly impossible to resist. One of the most insidious parts of this plan is that it often promotes products that are not designed to last. Planned obsolescence ensures that consumption of their goods will never end.

Shaping the public's desire benefits corporations as they profit from people replacing a product or buying a service over and over again. So how does successful marketing work as a tool of social control? The most significant way this functions as a tool of social control is to pull people into serious debt. Once you are sufficiently in debt you are a slave to the system. To maintain the illusion of your lifestyle, you are forced to work more and more in order to meet your payments. Your exhaustion from working and the fear of not fulfilling all of your financial obligations prevents you from having enough energy to question the insanity of the merry-go-round cycle of work and consume.

The competition for a limited number of jobs puts more pressure on you to stay on top of the trends, justifying your current or desired position at a company. Those around you become a source of anxiety. There is the boss who may be thinking, "Why should I keep you rather than hire the kid who just got all the latest training, will take lower pay, and is eager to work insane hours because he has no children?" Your neighbor has become a potential competitor for your job and status. At this point, you have been successfully converted into an isolated worker bee for the system, constantly in fear of everything falling apart.

To break free of this powerful form of social control requires the Sacred Revolutions' practice of simplicity. Here are some basics for you to start immediately: remove yourself from voluntary exposure to the desire-creating system, and get out of debt completely.

You cannot remove yourself completely from the influence of the system, but you can greatly minimize its effectiveness. You need to become critical of everything you watch, read, and see. Ask yourself questions such as these:

- What is the worldview of the movie you are watching promoting?
- In what light does the TV show you are watching present other people?
- How are women presented in the advertisements you see in public places?
- What are advertisements or salespeople saying you will gain by purchasing a product?

Do not let information into your brain unfiltered. Ask questions and refuse to be pacified! Be aware of how you are being shaped by the world around you.

Limit your exposure. The greatest propaganda tool is your television. Severely limiting or getting rid of your television set is one of the most significant acts of liberation you can make. There were years where I did not even have a TV device in my home. Currently, we have the ability to watch movies or TV shows through Netflix or iTunes. This allows me to selectively and critically watch shows as a more intentional act, as opposed to getting sucked into channel surfing. It also eliminates commercials. When my children were two and five we had cable television and we were very careful to make sure they were only watching things like

Public Television shows designed for children and the like. Then we decided to get rid of TV altogether. Almost overnight my children stopped asking for products they saw advertised. This really brought home to me how powerful television is, even when you are careful with what you view. This is especially true for children who are not capable of watching television critically yet.

Consider getting rid of commercial TV altogether. The primary things people fear they will miss if they get rid of it are the news and sports. The news today is more interested in presenting shock, entertainment, and fear than objective or informative content. The news fully participates in promoting the propaganda even if they may be unaware of it. After being away from this so-called news for a month, I noticed how much better I felt without it. I bet you will, too, and I challenge you to try it and find out.

Another key move is to stop going to the mall. The mall is like an interactive, 3D TV. It works to shape and support the agendas of a consumerist view of the world. They present you with a definition of what success looks like, and offer you what you need to look that way yourself. You are promised happiness if you buy this product or that service. Everything is enticing and designed to reach your core needs: acceptance, safety, power, and sex. To help you meet those needs in ways you cannot afford, easy credit comes to the rescue.

After you have been away from television and the mall for some time, you will be amazed at how ridiculous consumerism seems when you come in contact with it again. You will wonder how you ever thought this was so important. Why you thought it was so hard to leave. And then there is the concern that sets in when your realize how many people are still there, and how successfully it is shaping their thoughts, opinions, and attitudes.

As alternatives to the television and the mall, consider hanging out and talking with friends and family; reading;

listening to music or audiobooks; learning something you always wanted to do; or spending some time in quiet reflection and prayer. Some of the exhaustion that makes us feel like crashing in front of the TV actually comes from watching it. Activity is healthy and comes with many natural benefits.

Getting out of Debt

Debt forges the chains of slavery that keep people tied to the current system. They keep you bound to endless work, too exhausted to question the system, and leave you feeling helpless to change anything. You must break free from these chains in order to change.

By removing yourself from television and the mall—both of which manufacture desires for things that you do not need—you start to get a handle on the problem. This will help kill the urgent need you feel to consume things you cannot afford. Start saving up for items you buy so that you do not add to your debt. By taking the time to save first, you will also have time to make sure you really need the item and are not making an impulse buy. If you still think you need it after taking the time to save for it, then it is more likely to be a legitimate desire.

You also need to start a savings account. With a savings account in place, you can weather the ups and downs of life without needing to go into further debt. An emergency car repair will not need to go on the credit card. The more you can envision the chains of debt slavery, the more motivation you will have to be free of it.

It is important to get out from under your current debt as soon as possible. This will mean not adding to it, and making extra payments toward paying it back. There is no way to speak to your specific circumstance here, which is why becoming connected to a Sacred Community is so important. In a community, others can come alongside you, help identify the way forward, and help keep you accountable.

To be a revolutionary in the Sacred Revolution means you will have to give up the "dream" that the system has laid out for you—the one that everyone believes they are entitled to want and fulfill. This is the carrot that is being held out, keeping everyone running on the treadmill that empowers the Domination System and benefits those at the top. You must reject the carrot. In its place, we strive for shalom. Shalom is the vision of God and the end goal of the Sacred Revolution.

Getting out of debt will be one of the hardest things you will ever have to do. It will most likely require changes to how you live. This includes what and where you eat, what you drive and how much you drive, where you live, and how often you go to paid events. Be strong and vigilant. There is no way forward until you can break from the chains that bind you to empty desires.

The Second Anti-Revolution Tactic: Entertainment

Another challenge for the social engineers of the Domination System is how to keep all the worker bees content to keep doing their work. How do they keep people distracted from looking too closely at how things are run? This is accomplished through entertainment.

If you are relegated to a mundane job of repetitive actions for eight or more hours of the day, you will need some release when you get home. For many people, this comes in the form of watching television. Watching the bad guy get beat up, or the destruction of corporate buildings, becomes a cathartic release. Watching someone play out all the things we daydream about doing, but would never actually do, gives us a form of satisfaction. Sports gives us competition and something to rally behind. Knowing all the stats of our favorite team and defending their honor during the games is a near obsession for some people.

We also see people who are living the dream, either in fictional stories or reality TV. This reminds us of why we are working so hard. We think that if one day we could attain even a fraction of what we see on television we would be happy. Or people are depicted in such deplorable conditions or situations we are assured that our lives are not so bad.

Entertainment distracts us from paying attention to what is damaging our world, and asking important questions like who is causing that destruction. Entertainment distracts us from understanding what we believe. If we know more about our team's stats than we do about the Bible, how will we know if someone is misrepresenting our faith?

We have to recognize how entertainment is used against us and fight against getting sucked into it. That is not to say that relaxing and enjoying entertainment from time to time is bad, just that you have to be critical of what is being mentally consumed so that you do not mindlessly accept what you are fed. It also means being aware of entertainment's addictive nature so we are on guard from excessive amounts of distraction. We should make a determined effort to not subject ourselves to all the pacifying entertainment out there that contains no redeeming value.

The Third Anti-Revolution Tactic: Soundbite Communication

As a teacher of the Sacred Revolution, I am always wrestling with how to present material to my classes in the most effective way possible. When others offer their advice on how to do this, they usually suggest using sound bites or bullet points in order to engage those with shorter attention spans.

This is a common idea in marketing—from advertising to entertainment. A music video usually switches from image to image every few seconds in order to keep people engaged. Commercials compact information inside a minute to ensure their audience stays focused. But the most important things in life cannot be condensed into thirty second segments, and you need to refuse information fed to you this way. Why? Because "too long; didn't read" summaries and sound bites are a powerful tool for social control.

It is not by accident that everything happens so quickly today. Look at movies, television shows, and news channels. The camera perspective, colors, and sounds change very rapidly. This is especially true for media which targets the younger generation. Television has become the primary source of news, while newspapers are either failing or revamping to be more precise and to the point (sound bite news). So how is this control? Isn't this just using new technology to consume more information than ever before?

Two points need to be considered. First is the physiological, that what the brain does while watching television is different from what it does while reading. Watching television stimulates the pleasure center of the brain and is a passive activity. In addition, the flashing lights and changing camera angles become addictive to the point that it becomes harder for the viewer to watch something that is not constantly moving. This decreases the attention span in other normal activities in life.

Reading, in contrast, is a very active process in which the logic center of the brain is used to decode the symbols of the written word. The pleasure center is less discriminating regarding what comes through the senses, whereas the logic center is actively trying to understand that information. Visually addictive news can have the effect of pacifying the viewer to the point that apathy is practically an epidemic in our society. More information on this topic can be found in Al Gore's book, *The Assault on Reason*.

Second is that new ideas cannot be introduced in sound bites. You can only effectively communicate in sound bites if you keep to what your audience already understands. Trying to say something that might be outside the status quo will seem stupid. This is why talk shows are so effective. Someone calling in to disagree with the host does not have enough time to explain a contrary position. The host, who has their whole segment to make their point, will appear correct. Sound bites keep new ideas from emerging.

As a method of control, sound bites keep the masses passive and focused on the accepted way of viewing our lives. Sacred Revolutionaries are meant to be change-agents in this world. We cannot afford to be passive, and what God has to say to us is definitely going to be outside the world's "normal." We must listen to more than sound bites for information or else the Gospel will become distorted, no longer distinguishable from the world.

The Fourth Anti-Revolution Tactic: Labeling

Up to this point, all of the tactics of social control are dealing with people in general. This next tactic deals with people who hold ideological convictions. Religion can galvanize people together and allows them to possibly resist social norms. In days gone by they would burn heretics as a public display of what happens to dissenters. This was an effective means of dissuading others from following or even associating with those outside the accepted norm. Because we no longer find it appropriate to burn people alive, other social shaming techniques are used to prevent people from wanting to associate with dissenters of the norm. The primary tool to accomplish this is labeling.

People who go too far outside the norm are labeled radicalized. By labeling someone "radicalized" they are depicted as dangerous and irrational. This is how we talk about terrorists. As a country, we have considered radicals so dangerous that we have allowed them to be detained without charges or access to a lawyer. We have allowed what most would call torture, or at the very least cruel treatment, and undisclosed holding locations for "radicals." This is not to say that there are no real threats out there. There are enough examples of this kind of extreme danger that the public has accepted extreme measures to be used against those suspected of being a part of them. But these extreme measures open up the possible abuse of innocent people, and those responsible are beyond accountability. There are several documented cases of innocent individuals getting caught up in this system of interrogation because of their associations or ethnic origin, and there is no way for them to appeal unfair treatment. This is what makes labeling such a powerful tool. The risk of being labeled a radical, or showing up on some government watch list because of something you read or a seminar you attended, effectively controls the possibility of dissenting views from spreading.

It is not only the government that is concerned with variations from the norm. As you grow in your convictions and actions as a Sacred Revolutionary you will experience the same type of labeling and shaming from family and friends. Most of us have gone through a phase where our family or friends are uncomfortable with the idea of the Sacred Revolution. In their fear they will label you, your ideas, or your associates as "unorthodox" and "not Christian." They will challenge you by asking questions like, "Are you saying that the church your whole family goes to is wrong?" "What makes you think you have the truth and everyone else is wrong?" This can begin very early as you get excited about what you are learning and experiencing in the Sacred Revolution. Your excitement makes you want to share your new understanding with friends and family, but they might not be ready to hear it.

If this happens to you, remember that other's actions of labeling and shaming are because they are afraid. It is critical at this point that you work to reassure them of several thoughts.

First, you want to make it clear that you are not trying to convert them. What you are learning is committed to open dialog, never coercive, and absolutely nonviolent.

Second, this is not about "I am right and you are wrong." It is about opening up a conversation about differences in understanding. The differences provide an opportunity for exploring why we do what we do. Much of what we do in our life is not examined and those unexamined areas of life make up what we believe life is all about. When we are confronted with something different, it can challenge us at the level of, "that's just the way things are." That rocks someone's world to the core. If they are not on the same path of finding that level of understanding, they are not going to be happy about you shaking things up.

Third, you may consider not attempting to share everything right away. Sometimes people respond much better to seeing the differences rather than being told about them. Being involved in a community that is actively putting into practice the ways of the Sacred Revolution can speak far more powerfully that anything you can say.

THE SACRED REVOLUTION REVISTED

The future is before us, what are we going to make of it? Jesus has confronted us with God's radical vision of shalom. We have been invited to see the interconnectedness of everything and that our common well-being depends on respecting those relationships.

Following Jesus in the way of shalom places us in opposition to the way of the Domination System, a system that most of our world has become dependent on. The way of shalom envisions an alternative to the Domination System based on the three main priorities of gratitude, covenantal faithfulness, and community life. This is the call to the Sacred Revolution.

One of our challenges moving forward is how to relate to others who hold different religious beliefs than us or come from a more secular worldview. Historically, people have used these differences to justify everything from noncooperation to violence.

The more I reflect on the vision of shalom, the more I realize that the particular names or language we use to describe what we believe are not as important as what behavior our beliefs manifest. If someone's life reflects attributes that are consistent with God's vision of shalom, does it matter what language they use to explain it? I find that the life and call of Jesus speak powerfully to me, but for a growing number of people the church is failing to inspire participation and social transformation. Christianity has become problematic in its division, hate, and anti-intellectual positions that some have taken.

Doing the will of God does not require that people call their organization "Christian" or "Church". It is possible to be in an interdependent, healthy, accountable community that is doing the will of God without the individuals in that

169

community knowing if God exists or making a proclamation about the divinity of Jesus. God's will is fundamentally concerned with the realization of shalom for creation.

I know the preceding paragraph raises many questions for some people, especially about the necessity of Jesus and his work on the cross. These are important questions that I will continue to address in subsequent volumes. For now I will say Jesus' actions and what happened to him on the cross are directly related to his confrontation with the Domination System of his day, which modeled for us how we follow in his way. Jesus said, "Whoever does not carry the cross and follow me cannot be my disciple" (Luke 14:27).

Consider what the Apostle Paul had to say about non-believing Gentiles who act in the way the people of God should, even though the Gentiles were not a part of Paul's faith:

> When Gentiles, who do not possess the law, do instinctively what the law requires, these, though not having the law, are a law to themselves. They show that what the law requires is written on their hearts, to which their own conscience also bears witness; and their conflicting thoughts will accuse or perhaps excuse them on the day when, according to my gospel, God, through Jesus Christ, will judge the secret thoughts of all.
> (Romans 2:14-16)

This passage opens up interesting possibilities for how we collaborate with others of different faith positions. The core of the Sacred Revolution provides a view that is sufficiently broad to incorporate people from many different perspectives. Our witness as a living alternative is what will spark the conversation about alternate, or deeper, possibilities in faith and living. Before that change in our own lives, it is all just arguing about ideas, and the side of worldly normal will win because the lived experience will always carry more weight than the hypothetical. If you are called to be a Sacred Revolutionary, God has given you the gift of making that hypothetical God-given vision of shalom into a reality that will enable others to follow.

I am proposing the following manifesto as a guide for how we might move forward in building a future in God's vision of shalom.

THE SACRED REVOLUTION MANIFESTO

Stories

The world is a beautiful and mysterious place, full of possibilities and abundance. It is an intricate, balanced network of life. Counter to this natural balance are systems of domination and waste that produce lives filled with hopelessness, brutality, and hunger. These darker influences are interwoven into cultures all over the planet, making it difficult to imagine a world without them.

Systems of domination and waste are a consequence of desires shaped by faulty perceptions of the world and our place in it. Perceptions can be changed. Our perceptions are formed by stories that give meaning and direction to life. Humans are storied creatures. We think in the form of narratives. Even our most scientific understandings are communicated as a story. Our foundational stories present us with a vision of the world and shape our desires and actions.

Some stories form a perspective of our place on Earth as being part of creation, with us striving to live in harmony and balance. Other stories form an image of the Earth as a resource, meant to be exploited for our own purposes. The stories that we allow to form our minds and the minds of our children have the power to change our world.

We need to rid ourselves of stories that speak of Earth as a mechanized system, good only as a source of profit. Instead, imagine a story of interconnectedness and enoughness that leaves us at harmony with the Earth. The stories of us versus them need to be replaced with the story of we. The stories of peace through violence needs to be replaced with the story of peace through reconciliation. This story is the story of the Sacred Revolution.

Humanity no longer has the luxury to simply separate from those who differ in thinking. We must engage in the demanding work of resolving differences. The impact of human activity in this world has become so massive that some stories being told threaten the health and security of everyone on the planet. Therefore, the stories we tell, and the way of life they produce, should be everyone's concern.

Religions have powerful stories that influence their followers, but religion can also create dividing walls and hostility between people of different faiths. Some have tried to overcome religious division by claiming that all religions essentially teach the same thing. This is not true and is disrespectful to the unique teachings that each faith offers. The Sacred Revolution seeks to find common ground in areas that most faiths and non-religious people can agree on, while celebrating our unique differences as vital to the richness of life.

The story of the Sacred Revolution has been largely shaped by the life and teachings of Jesus; however, we do not fall neatly into a "Christian" package. We are excited to find areas of commonality with others rather than focusing on division. This manifesto is designed to be maximally inclusive, allowing us to work together for the common good.

Definitions

THE SACRED: Reflecting on the mysteries of life fills us with a sense of awe as we consider the ultimate Source of life and being. This feeling of awe is the experience of approaching the sacredness of the Source. The Source has been given many different names by religion or science, and people have developed unique practices of respecting it. The origin of the word sacred means "to be separate," and we use sacred to describe people, time, places, and things which are connected to the Source. That is, they are set apart from what is commonplace and are more closely related to the Source.

REVOLUTION: The origin of the word revolution mean "to turn around," as in revolve, and applies to turning around systems of human organization. Most of our experience of revolutions involve the violent overturning of governments. By referring to our movement as a Sacred Revolution, we mean to show that our revolution is not one of violence, but of peace.

DOMINATION SYSTEM: Massive inequality of wealth, justice, and resources are typical in systems of domination. These systems use violence and propaganda to legitimize inequality. Oppression, brutality, and hopelessness are the experiences of those at the bottom of the system. It is no better at the top, as they experience a lack of satisfaction and sensitivity for those below them. When a few benefit at the expense of the many, you have a domination system.

WASTE SYSTEM: Waste is foreign to the natural systems of creation. Within the Earth's ecosystem there is no waste, as everything cycles back as food or a resource to another part of the system. Everything has value. This is how it must be to sustain life in a limited system. Waste systems create byproducts that are toxic, unusable, and destroy the environment. Waste systems typically depend on continual growth and therefore promote chronic overconsumption.

LOVE AND COMPASSION: When Jesus called his followers to love their enemies, he was not expecting them to feel a strong emotional attachment to them, but that they would not dehumanize their enemies. Loving an enemy means that we remember we are all connected; therefore, we must struggle to find alternative ways of addressing wrongs rather than defaulting to the use of violence or retribution. Compassion means to feel for one another and to empathize with what someone else is experiencing.

Affirmations

FIRST: We recognize and respect the sacred in everything. All of life and creation are a gift from the ultimate Source and everything in our world is interconnected and interdependent in countless ways. This is the fundamental shift in the stories we tell and all that follows is a consequence of seeing the sacred in everything. This would seem to be in contradiction to the definition of sacred, "to be separate." The separateness of the sacred comes from a human desire to keep the purity of the Source clean from the dirtiness we experience in life; however, the dirtiness of life is the result of a failure to recognize the sacred in everything. When we view a person, place, or thing as common, it is easier to misuse it than if we recognize it as sacred.

Recognizing the sacred in everything has a profound effect on our perception of the world and our interactions with it and each other. Caring for creation is vital to our existence, as is having respect for all people including those who have wronged us. We must learn to see the sacred in ourselves, as we are also a part of the whole.

SECOND: We honor the diversity of religious and philosophical perspectives to the degree that they affirm life and reject violence as a means to an end. We listen to others' experiences of the sacred, allowing it to expand our understanding in beautiful ways.

THIRD: We acknowledge that our well-being is directly dependent on the well-being of all others.

FOURTH: We are led to alleviate the suffering of people and end the destruction of creation brought about by systems of domination and waste. This is because we recognize and respect the sacred in all things.

FIFTH: We commit to nonviolent action in working to alleviate suffering and destruction. A commitment to nonviolence is essential if we are to avoid replacing one system of domination with another.

SIXTH: We seek the redemption and reconciliation of our oppressors, or enemies, rather than their destruction. We see those caught up in running systems of domination and waste as in need of rescue as much as those who are victims of the systems.

SEVENTH: We choose to utilize love and compassion as tools in dismantling systems of domination and waste.

THE SACRED REVOLUTION MANIFESTO IN ONE SENTENCE

Respecting the sacred in everything leads us to dismantle systems of domination and waste through nonviolent action guided by love and compassion.

Made in the USA
San Bernardino, CA
01 July 2016